Religions of India

Religions of India

◆

A User Friendly and Brief Introduction to Hinduism, Buddhism, Sikhism, and the Jains

Jack Sikora

Writers Club Press
San Jose New York Lincoln Shanghai

Religions of India
A User Friendly and Brief Introduction to Hinduism, Buddhism, Sikhism, and the Jains

Writers Club Press
an imprint of iUniverse, Inc.

For information address:
iUniverse, Inc.
5220 S. 16th St., Suite 200
Lincoln, NE 68512
www.iuniverse.com

Hinduism, Buddhism, Sikhism, Jain Religion

ISBN: 0-595-24712-1

Printed in the United States of America

This book is for Lynn, Beth, Tempe, and Caroline and for my teachers, especially H. Daniel Smith and the late Truman "A plus" Warner

Contents

Preface

This book is very much a product of a number of years of teaching both graduate and undergraduate students about the religious traditions, peoples, and cultures of India and Southeast Asia. I am especially indebted to my students, both past and present especially "C.J." for showing me how to teach more effectively, and it is their collective wisdom that has guided my hand in preparing this small volume. It is they that continue to tell me "what works" toward helping them to best understand and ultimately appreciate a corpus of subject matter that is at once arresting, inspiring, yet also bewildering and often intimidating. If I have succeeded in making this book a helpful and friendly vehicle for learning, then I have my students to thank. Where I have failed I have only myself to blame.

I must also thank my colleagues, especially Professors Jerry Bannister and Jack Leopold, in the Departments of Social Science and History at Western Connecticut State University who facilitated for me significant opportunities to develop courses in Asian religions both on campus and "online." These "champions" of intercultural learning have done much to carry forth the work of the late Professor Truman Warner to make Western a vital locus for the study of non-Western cultures.

Further, I owe a special debt of gratitude to the Graduate Liberal Studies Program at Wesleyan University where I have served as a visiting faculty member. My student colleagues, supervisors, and the staff at Wesleyan have enabled me to grow professionally under their kindly wings and in the splendid beauty of their campus while inspiring me to continue to learn to teach more effectively.

Special thanks to Elisabeth Sikora Labriola, my student, my daughter, and the fine artist whose work graces the cover of this book. Last

but not least, I thank my dear life-long friend, Professor Pauline Keat-
ing Arneberg for her unflagging nurture.

JS
Old Saybrook, Connecticut
August 2002

1

Introduction to the Hindu Tradition

The following are some general observations to help you develop an overview for Hinduism and other Indian religions such as that of the Jains and the Sikhs. Please note that throughout this book when I present important terms/concepts I use italics and/or "bullets" and write the information in **bold** to help you focus and attend to essential information.

The religious tradition we call Hinduism is the product of 5,000 years of development. The term Hinduism dates from around 1200 C.E. when invaders used the term "Hindu" to mean either:

1. The Hindu Way or religious tradition
2. Original/indigenous population of Hind (India)
3. The religion of the original people of India
4. Non-Muslims

Hinduism is also sometimes called Brahmanism because it was taught/controlled by brahmans.

brahmans—**Ancient priestly caste; brahmans were/are religious specialists (priests).**

Unlike Buddhism, Sikhism, Judaism, Christianity, or Islam, for example, Hinduism was not founded by an individual. While the Hindu tradition has numerous significant "saints" and pundits, it has no principal prophets, is generally unstructured (unlike a Church), and has no established "creed" that might serve to underscore a unified set

1

of common beliefs or identify more or less precisely what distinguishes a "Hindu" per se. Indeed the Hindu way constitutes numerous and often quite diverse beliefs and practices. Nevertheless, there exists within the numerous large and small tributaries that flow in the vast sea of Hinduism certain common elements of tradition, belief, and practice that most Hindus and students of Hinduism might readily recognize as characterizing the Hindu Way. It is these elements that this book addresses.

In Hinduism there is an emphasis is on the way in which one lives. Perhaps for that reason Hinduism has been described as more like a set of cultural principles and practices or legalistic prescriptions and proscriptions than a religion. Indeed, some Hindus prefer to describe Hinduism in terms of "right action" or "duty" called **dharma.**

dharma—**Eternal teaching/law or "that which has been given."**

In order to avoid confusion later, you may wish to note here that *dharma* in the Hindu context has specific meaning(s) related to "right" action which differ from the concept(s) of Dharma in Buddhism.

Some important additional beliefs held by most Hindus are: *samsara, atman, karma,* and *moksha.* To help us grasp these concepts we might recognize first that Hindus think of the flow of life as passing through many existences. This is called *samsara.*

samsara—**"The course." This concept refers to the path(s) taken by the "spirit" in its many rebirths and reincarnations in different bodies and forms (human, animal, vegetable, etc).**

atman; jiva; and *purusa*—**These are terms used to describe the "spirit" or essence that is reborn/transmigrated. Atman is most commonly used and may be translated and understood as the "self."**

It is very important for you to understand that the fate of the atman running the course of samsara is determined by the accumulation of good and/or bad karma. For now we will define karma in these terms:

karma—**The consequences of one's works, deeds, and actions.**

Samsara is a central concern for Hindus. Release from the endless round of samsara is the spiritual goal of Hindus who seek **moksha**, ultimate release and its resulting blissful peace.

moksha or *mukti*—**The concept of release from samsara; moksha is not equivalent to the Western term/concept of "salvation;" however, out of convenience many writers (including this one) will employ the term "salvation" to indicate moksha, Nirvana, or some other ultimate spiritual goal.**

Hinduism has a great and vast corpus of sacred literature. The following concepts are foundational to understanding Hindu sacred writings:

scruti—**"That which has been heard." All Hindu scriptures that are regarded as "revealed" truth and which cannot be argued. The Vedas fall into this category.**

smrti—**"That which is remembered." Smrti can be argued/ contradicted. Smrti is sacred writing, but it is not scripture. The sacred books of the religious law such as the *Manava Dharma Sastra_(Laws of Manu)* fall into this category.**

Let's now turn to a brief, general view of India. Traditional India was isolated and agricultural. The oceans to the east and west and the Himalayan Range to the north contributed to India's relative isolation. Thus its religious traditions developed with little outside influence even in the face of the Mughul conquests and the British Raj. Although no longer isolated, India remains agricultural. Agriculture is enhanced by the presence of fertile plains, the significant effect of rivers, and the monsoon rains in the south.

A point to remember is that rivers are understood by Hindus to be particularly important in religious life. Two rivers hold special significance for many Hindus, the Ganges and the Jumna:

Ganges—This sacred river is rich in spiritual significance and symbolism. It represents eternal life.

Jumna—This river, too, has significant spiritual importance.

Largely because of it location near the rivers, the sacred city of Varanasi is of great spiritual significance:

Varanasi (Benares/Banaras)—The most holy city of Hinduism; situated on the Ganges River; it is the most sacred place in which to die and from which to have one's cremains scattered in the Ganges.

Finally, please appreciate that the points covered in this Chapter are but a "bare bones introduction to a complex and awe inspiring subject. You will find additional bibliographical references at the end of this book. I encourage you to investigate, enjoy, and employ them along with the material presented here.

2

Indus Civilization, Aryan Religion & The Vedas

I ndus religion and other South Asian indigenous traditions appear to have influenced to varying degrees Hinduism, Buddhism, Jainism and other Indian religious Ways. Indeed, some scholars argue that there is a dual origin for Hinduism, i.e. Indus culture and its religion and the Vedas. In this Chapter we will seek to explore further the nature of the relationship of Hindu beliefs and practices and Indus religion. Please note that Jain religion, which we will consider later, also seems to have inherited from Indus religion a tradition that includes meditation and special sacred places.

Indus culture and Hinduism

The Indus Valley Civilization is sometimes called Harappa, the name of one of its cities. Indus Civilization (Harappa) dates from approximately 2700 to 1500 B.C.E.. Because Indus writing remains undeciphered, what we know about it is largely based on the artifacts and archaeological sites so far discovered. To date about 200 towns and large cities have been uncovered (at least in part) including two major cities, Harappa and Mohenjo-daro. Most of our understanding of the culture comes from the excavated sites and the depictions of various figures carved onto soapstone seals that seem to have been associated with trade and perhaps ritual.

In part because some scholars theorize that there is a "dual origin" for Hinduism, i.e. the Vedas and the culture of the Indus Civilization, the following points in summary are worthy of our attention regarding Indus Civilization:

- the excavations reveal remarkable city planning and sanitation (wells provided household water; houses had bathrooms and latrines which were capable of being flushed)

- temple citadels suggest sacred kingship and thus some kind of synthesis of religion and the state

- ritual purity seems to have been important , and ritual bathing occurred (in Hinduism water holds a prominent spiritual place as does ritual purification with water)

- The seal engravings are significant to our knowledge of Indus culture, and the seals suggest, among a number of things, that:

1. There seems to have been goddess worship, specifically worship of a "mother" goddess

2. A possible tradition associated with meditation as revealed in the image of a male figure in a "yogic" lotus position

3. A horned "god" on the seals may be a "proto" Siva

4. Trees and animals (in particular bulls) may have had sacred significance

5. There is evidence of phallic worship (you may discern the significance of this in modern worship of the god Siva)

Thus the significance of Indus culture for our purposes is that the Hindu tradition seems to have some deeply indigenous roots in the region we now call South Asia. Specifically, numerous elements of Hindu belief and practice seem to have origins in Indus culture, e.g. meditation, goddess worship, Siva worship, the importance of water, etc. Where this leads in terms of "understanding" Hinduism is the subject of much debate far beyond the scope of this book, but at the very least we might do well to appreciate that the religious ways that became Hinduism are perhaps not entirely a result of outside influences such as Aryan religion. By 1600 B.C.E. the Indus Civilization was virtually gone. Why? We aren't sure, but some reasons have been suggested such as crop failure, flood, drought, depletion of wood, disease, and Aryan "conquest."

The Aryans

As we have noted there may be a dual origin for Hinduism, i.e. in Indus culture and the Vedas, but some scholars argue that other indigenous traditions also played a significant role as well. These other traditions include folk religion and localized myths and practices, but certainly Aryan culture and religion are without much doubt a major factor in the development of the Hindu way, and we will now focus upon these ancient people and their *Vedas*, the most sacred of Hindu scriptures.

Please note that I will be using the term **worldview** in this book; therefore, allow me to momentarily depart from our discussion in order to offer a simplified definition of this term:

> **Worldview—A culture's characteristic way of perceiving, interpreting, and explaining the world.**

First, let's appreciate that the Aryans should not to be confused with the evil concept of a so-called "Aryan Race" aspired to by Hitler and the Nazis.

> **Arya/Aryan—Caucasian people who "invaded" India around 2000B.C.E. and whose language and culture were assimilated by the indigenous people**

Most of what we know about the Aryans comes from the Vedas, but some scholars also argue that, based on linguistic and other data, that the Aryans "originated" in the present Central Europe and ranged from the Baltic regions to present day Poland. Their territory eventually extended into the steppe lands of Central Asia. They began to migrate around 2000 B.C.E..

Some of the social and cultural characteristics that both distinguish the Aryans and speak to their capacity to dominate by conquest and/or assimilation the indigenous culture(s) of India were their technological resources, especially horses, chariots, and iron weapons. A society of warrior-like pastoralists they worshipped sky and other nature gods, were organized politically into patriarchal tribal units, and had a strong oral tradition that included hymns in praise of their deva(s).

deva(s)—**Extrahuman powers and/or gods.**

Aryan society was stratified into three hierarchical social ranks, i.e. brahmans (priests), warriors, and all others.

Once in India the Aryas further developed and refined their Sanskrit language.

Sanskrit—The language of the Aryan peoples. Sanskrit is an Indo-European language related to Latin, Greek, and Persian. It is the sacred language of the Hindu scriptures.

scripture—Writings which are believed to be divinely inspired or especially authoritative within a particular religious community.

The Vedas

The Vedas are scripture and are classified as sruti.

Vedas—"Corpus of knowledge." Collections of Aryan hymns, ritual prescriptions, and sacred speculations. The scriptures which express the religion of the Aryans.

The Vedas are believed to contain revelations given to the ancient sages (Rishis) directly from an eternal source. The following are points that might help you appreciate the power and significance of the Vedas:

1. The Sanskrit in which the Vedas are recited and preserved is sacred and holy because of its association with the Vedas

2. The Vedic verses are so holy that to hear them or to be instructed in them is reserved for the "twice-born," the three highest varnas (caste-related) ranks in the hierarchical caste system which we will discuss and explain further later

3. Sudras (lower caste people), untouchables, and women are ordinarily forbidden access to the Vedas

The Vedas are categorized into four divisions as follows:

I. Rigveda—Hymns to the Aryan gods, who generally appear as personifications of natural forces.

II. Samaveda—Special chants for ritual purposes.

III. Yajurveda—Instructions for ritual (a manual for conducting rituals).

IV. Arthaveda—Ritualized spells and incantations usually focused on healing.

The Rigveda is the oldest of the Veda. Scholars date it from around 1,500 to 1000 B.C.E.. There are 1,028 hymns in the Rigveda. A hymn is usually addressed to a single deity, but several different gods may be addressed in a hymn. The most important deity in the Rigveda is Indra.

The Samaveda are essentially technical texts and formulae for use in ritual. The Samaveda "samars" (songs) are based on the Rigveda. The Yajurveda are also technical texts and formulae for ritual. They are used by an adhvaryu (a priest specializing in the physical preparation and offerings at a sacrifice). The Artharvaveda is very ancient. It consists mainly of spells and incantations with a general focus on healing. The Artharvaveda is less concerned with ritual and addresses the problems of ordinary life. Artharvan priests are brahmans who specialize in healing and counseling.

The principal deva(s) (gods) of the Vedas are:

Varuna—His domain is the sky; the god of rita (which we will discuss later); omnipresent; always aware of the deeds of humans; punishes "sinners"

Indra—Warrior god of Aryans; god of thunder; inhabits the atmosphere

Vishnu—A relatively minor god in the early Vedas, but in later Hinduism he is vastly significant; associated with the sun and highest heaven

Rudra—Also called Siva/Shiva (who is extremely important in later Hinduism); he is known as the "howler;" called "auspicious;" he is associated with destruction and the prevention of destruction

Agni—Fire god; god of the home; intermediary between gods and humans; intimately connected with the fire sacrifice (which we will discuss later).

Vedic Worldview and Hinduism

Now let's consider the Vedic worldview and prepare the way for addressing further the seminal concepts of *rita, dharma*, and *karma.* Essentially the Vedic worldview of the Aryans was practical, i.e. to get the gods to give one what one wants/needs by coercing and "capturing" the extrahuman, the cosmic powers and the gods themselves. The Aryans were a warrior people, a lusty lot focused on maximizing earthly life. There was little concern with transcendence and a different level of existence. The Aryan notion of "heaven" is a "party place," a locus of conviviality, feasting, fighting and wenching in the presence and with the good company of the departed, but otherwise the afterworld was not clearly defined in the Aryan cosmology and worldview. The Aryans were principally focused on the here and now and the fullness of life.

The Vedic universe was divided into three realms established by the god Vishnu. These realms were:

I. Earth (terrestrial)

II. Realm of birds and chariots of gods (atmospheric)

III. Realm of deities and the dead (celestial)

The gods were divided into the three classes depending on the realm in which they were principally located and where they acted, i.e. sky, atmosphere, or earth.

The Aryans believed that the life essence was centered on the breath, i.e. prana.

prana—"Breath;" the basic animating principle; connected with atman.

atman—"self;" a subtle substance residing in the body but separate from it.

Just as prana was believed to be central to life, rita was the force that sustained creation, and the god Varuna oversaw it; however, Varuna was not its creator nor sustainer. He was its guardian only. All things, all powers, all creation including the gods were governed by the force of rita.

rita or *rta*—The impersonal principle of ethical and physical organization of the universe; rita maintains cosmic and human order; rita enables human harmony.

Rita was believed to enable peace, justice, and order even to the degree that it made possible the pattern of correct ritual performance, and correct ritual performance maintained harmony between humans, nature, and the gods.

Rita is closely related to but not the same as dharma.

dharma—Refers to the law and the idea of righteousness that upholds the universe in both cosmic and mundane ways;

"dharma" derives from a verbal root "dhr" meaning to "uphold;" "to hold steady;" or "to preserve."

In understanding Hinduism, it is useful to think of dharma as "duty." In Hinduism, the dharma (duty) of one person differs from the dharma of another depending upon one's caste affiliation, stage of life, local conventions, etc, i.e. in the Sanskrit this is called *dharmavarnaashrama*. We will discuss this further later on. For now you may wish to note that dharma does not change over time. One's sacred duty (dharma) is an eternal duty.

Dharma is intimately connected to *karma*.

***karma*—The effect of former deeds/misdeeds (performed either in this life or a former one) on one's present and future condition**

It is through karma that the form or corporal body of the next life (divine, human, animal, etc) is acquired. Previous karma "creates" a person's character, fortune, social class/caste, happiness and sorrow. Every good act brings its result sooner or later in happiness. Every evil act brings sorrow. Hindus believe that through effort over the courses of many incarnations one can master and overcome one's evil tendencies and control one's karma.

Vedic Sacrifice

The Aryans brought with them the practice of sacrifice. Along with the sacrifice and, as an essential part of the sacrificial rites, the Aryans developed a rich religious oral tradition. Priests ultimately perfected their techniques used for the hymns that were sung in praise of the devas at the sacrifice. Indeed, precise recitation of hymns (Vedas) was (and continues to be) central to the sacrifice. The hymns, properly executed created sacred sounds that captured the essence of the gods. The power of the devas was thereby entrapped by the priests (brahmans) and ensured the efficacy of the sacrifice. Thus, the Vedas, in addition to being extremely sacred, are also very powerful, powerful enough to enable mortals to entice and hold the gods themselves. Their place in Hinduism cannot be understated.

The sacrificial offerings of the Aryans included animals, grain, ghee (clarified butter), spices, and soma (probably the fermented juice of a plant or fungus and which had intoxicating and even perhaps hallucinogenic effects).

The sacrifice itself was generally centered around a fire and offered on behalf of a patron and in honor of one or several devas. As the fire burned the Vedas were recited in order to petition for particular favors from the gods. Patrons might ask for such things as long life, many cattle, sons, etc. Over time the sacrifice became associated with the maintenance of the cosmos itself and it continues to be performed to assure that creation remains, albeit fragile, intact.

Precision in all aspects of the sacrificial rites was critical. If the rites were not performed precisely they would be ineffective and/or the gods might be offended and dangerous consequences might befall the patron of the sacrifice as well as the priests. For this reason, over time several ritual specialists (brahman priests) took on institutionalized roles to assist with the sacrifice to the extent that eventually a kind of priest took on the role of watching the other priests to ensure precision.

In the Arya Yajna cult fire sacrifice and elsewhere the god Agni played an important role. Agni was the personification of sacrificial fire and Agni linked heaven and earth; therefore, as a kind of "messenger" of the gods, Agni carried to the petitioned god the sacrificial gifts which the brahmans pour into the flames.

Among the Aryans (and modern day Hindus) sacrificial rites were conducted by both priests and householders. The following terms describe and differentiate these rites:

griha—**Domestic rites performed by a householder.**

srauta—**Rituals performed by brahman priests**

It is useful to note that while evolutionary development of the fire sacrifice expanded the role and power of priests, the status of the householder and his role in worship is an ongoing principle central to the practice of the Hindu Way. Thus in general Hinduism is less a community centered religion and more an individual one. Brahman priests are repositories of priestly knowledge and keepers of Brahman (power, truth, prayer, the very "sacred" itself), but they serve as religious specialists on behalf of individuals.

In the next Chapter we will learn more about brahmans and their role in the Hindu Way.

3

The Brahmanical Tradition: Upanishads, Sutras, and Dharma Literature

The Hindu way includes three principal *marga(s)* (paths to "salvation" or moksha), and they are individualistic, personal, non-communally oriented. The three principal classic margas are: 1) *jnanamarga*—Way of Knowledge; 2) *karmamarga*—Way of Action; 3)*bhaktimarga*—Way of Devotion. In this Chapter we will examine the Upanishads as *jnanamarga*, the way of knowledge or truth and what these scriptures and the worldview and related practices reveal about the development of Hinduism and the emergence of the caste system. Then we will to the Dharma Sutras and Dharma Sastras to glean some understanding of *kharmamarga* and its place in the Hindu tradition. Let's begin with the concept of caste and its role in the Brahmanical tradition and later Hinduism.

You will recall that Aryan social stratification consisted of priests, warriors, and all others. But by the end of the Vedic period society was divided into four categories called *varna.*

> *varna*—Literally means "color;" refers to the fourfold division of society based loosely on occupation and which defines religious status and prescriptive roles and proscriptions.

The notion of varna speaks to the Bramanical belief that a hierarchical social structure is divinely ordained and thus a part of the natural order of things, i.e. that it is right and maintains the right order of things in the heavens and upon the earth. Indeed, its maintenance preserves creation itself. Over time the varnas proliferated into a myriad jatis (birth groups) which were differentiated in terms of division of labor. Thus, there are now in India thousands of castes in addition to groups of people classified as outcastes and/or untouchables, the latter are associated with highly "polluting" work such as cleaning human waste, washing women's menstrual clothes, tanning cow hides, etc.

The first (uppermost) three varnas (which are comprised of thousands of castes) are:

1. **brahmana**
2. **ksyatriya**
3. **vaisya**

The brahmana or brahmans, ksyatriya, and vaishya are referred to as the "twice born" (dvijas) by virtue of sacramental (samskara) initiation including investiture with the sacred thread. In this sense they are "sacramentally" fully human; therefore, the twice born are distinguished from the castes under the fourth varna category of **sudra** as well as all other castes and outcasts. Some scholars suggest that the sudra were regarded as inferior based upon an alleged darker skin color, and, consequently, these castes cannot hope for moksha (release from samsara) until a future life when they are reborn among the twice born. Generally the traditional hereditary occupations ascribed to the varnas are: brahmans (priests); ksyatriya (warriors); vaisya (farmers); sudras (laborers).

Now let's consider the concept of caste.

caste—In Hindu society it is a system of social stratification based on hierarchical considerations derived from beliefs regarding such things as an individual's religious and ritual purity, ascribed status based on birth, traditional occupation and the like.

As a system of social stratification, the traditional Hindu caste system is maintained by more or less strict endogamy (marriage within the caste), rigid commensality (norms dictating such things as who may eat, touch, share utensils, etc, with whom), and adherence to other religious practices such as those described in the dharma texts, e.g. *Manu*, which we will discuss later.

The Upanishads

If we parse the term, we discover that the word upanishad is formed in the Sanskrit as follows:

upa = *"near"*

ni = *"down"*

Shad = *"sit"*

Thus "upanishad" = "to sit down near." Indeed, the upanishads are traditionally viewed in Hinduism as secret or semi-secret teachings, secret enough that a student should sit down near his guru (teacher) to hear, discourse, and learn the powerful and sacred mysteries. Traditionally, upsanishadic learning was restricted to the twice born brahmans who were believed to be sufficiently pure and able to receive it.

*upanishad(s)—refers to a broadly-ranging and miscellaneous body of speculative treatises composed in the early post-Vedic period (600–200 B.C.E.); later in the development of the Hindu way, certain upanishads came to be viewed as having captured the essence of the Vedic truth and are therefore sometimes referred to as vedanta (the "end" or culmination of the vedas).

The upanishads center on jnana.

*jnana—"Knowledge;" or as in the Greek concept of "gnosis," secret wisdom taught by sages from mystical experiences not available to ordinary people.

Neither jnana nor the upanishads are much concerned with outward ritual or social duty. Note how the focus is away from sacrifice and/or concerns with dharma. The upanishadic gurus were not involved with petitioning or "capturing" the devas or their powers nor with ritual sacrifice. They were concerned instead with discovering the basis of the universe, i.e. the Absolute Reality (Brahman), the very root of all things, that which was before existence came to be and which continues after existence ceases. The gurus taught that the fruits of sacrifice had no lasting worth. Of greater interest to them was exploring the nature and the power of human consciousness. Generally, the upanishads teach the reality of samsara and instruct that moksha or mukti (release) may be realized when the atman (self) is understood to be at one with and not different from the universal spirit of Brahman.

atman—self; in upanishadic teachings the atman is the inner, undying self which is identical to and continuous with the Supreme Identity or Ultimate Reality, i.e. Brahman or Brahm.

Brahman—the divine, Absolute Reality; the term/concept also originally referred to the holy power evoked through sacrifice and thus connotes the power of the cosmos itself.

The term "Brahman" also refers to the mysterious power comprehended when hearing the recitation of the Vedic hymns. In this sense Brahman "describes" the sacred words of the Veda which are experienced as a single power embracing all things is creation and in the universe beyond creation. A central teaching of the upanishads is that atman is identical to Brahman, i.e. the self is one with the divine, and this is the goal of spiritual realization, to recognize "*tat tvam asi*" (thou art that), i.e. that atman is Brahman and that the individual self finds "release" only when it loses itself in or merges with the Absolute. In this view, to know Brahman is to find one's being within Brahman, and this "knowledge" is *moksha*, release, liberation from the endless round of rebirths and sufferings inherent in samsara, and this is the goal of the upanishadic seekers such as the *sannyasi*. Moksha is the sincere desire of the sannyasi.

Sannyasi—"one who renounces;" someone who seriously studies vedanta (the teachings derived from the upanishads and believed by many Hindus to be the "essence" or "truth" of the Vedic revelations; a person who meditates in an introverted state in order to apprehend reality wherein there is liberation from all distress and peace in the realization of oneness with Brahman (samadhi).

The Upanishads center on *jnana*.

jnana—"Knowledge;" or as in the Greek concept of "gnosis," secret wisdom taught by sages from mystical experiences not available to ordinary people.

As we noted in the above neither jnana nor the upanishads center on ritual or social duty. The upanishadic gurus were not involved with petitioning or "capturing" the devas or their powers nor with ritual sacrifice. They were concerned instead with discovering the basis of the universe, i.e. the Absolute Reality (Brahman), the very root of all things, that which was before existence came to be and which continues after existence ceases. The gurus taught that the fruits of sacrifice had no lasting worth. Of greater interest to them was exploring the nature and the power of human consciousness. Certain upanishads, e.g. *Maitri, Svetasvatara* , etc promote yoga as a way to union with Brahman. There are a variety of "systems" of yoga which span a diverse practices involving meditation and control of mind and body. The term *yogi* or *yogin* refers to a practitioner of yoga.

Sutras

Sometime between 300 B.C.E. and 300 C.E. the brahmans invented the *sutra* as a vehicle for developing expositions on morality, values, and social norms.

sutra—Class of Sanskrit literature composed in a style so abbreviated that the texts generally require expansion and elaboration in the form of commentaries or oral expositions to render their "real" meaning; sutras are acknowledged to be imperfect documents subject to rational analysis and free inquiry.

Sutras may be so utterly brief as to involve serious misunderstanding unless elucidated by a guru or other competent preceptor. Thus sutras are viewed by orthodox Hindus as smriti. Examples of categories of sutras are:

grihyasutras—Discourses on domestic rites; prescriptions on how the householder should perform domestic rituals in the home.

Karmamarga—Prescriptions and proscriptions on social duty (dharma).

dharmashastras—elaboration on dharmasutras; detailed prescriptions on duty (dharma) of each varna and age group (asrama).

Dharma Literature & Dharmamarga

The following is an excerpt from an unpublished manuscript *A Dharma Reader: An Introduction to the Sacred Law of the Hindus* by H. Daniel Smith and Jack Sikora. It will provide you with a foundation for appreciating the dharmasutras/dharmasastras, especially *The Laws of Manu:*

> *According to Hindu tradition, the world is an ordered place. Deeds have consequences; society reveals a dynamic, interrelated, but ranked, hierarchy...human temporality finds its analogy in an expanded, divine time; and all things are subject to termination, decay or disintegration, only to be repeated, recreated and reconstructed in endless cycles...as the seasons repeat themselves, as the planets continue to*

wheel in their courses, as the human spirit is reincarnated again and again in countless rebirths, as the social order disintegrates toward a final cataclysm only to be reconstituted again in a new age, as the gods themselves live and die and are reborn, and as the universe itself traces out an ordained, cyclical destiny.

At least two classic responses to this view have been advanced. One response has been to regard the succession of worldly events negatively, that is, to see samsara…as a problem. This attitude suggests that life and the world is something to be eschewed, escaped…The other response has been to regard what transpires on the worldly plane positively…to see the cosmic course of samsara as a potential field for spiritual renewal and growth…The aim here is to assume one's worldly role actively, to acknowledge one's mundane duties gratefully, to work as an integral member of the body politic responsibly…The most eloquent testimony to this view is the concept of dharma itself…One who lives according to dharma is the one who, in his own way and despite his limitations, upholds the nature of things…

The genius of the dharmasastra writers was that their vision of the good life integrated both responses…but for the ordinary Hindu…what was encountered was a plenum of detailed dicta of specific rules for particular people in special circumstances…

For the most part the "order" that the the dharmasastra vision affirms has to do with the four-fold varna categories of brahmin, kshatriya, vaisya and sudra, with the purity of these ranked categories and with the permissible degrees of mixing their respective personnel, privileges and responsibilities; with the four-fold scheme of asrama-stages during which appropriate persons are sequentially students, householders, renunciates and anchorites, and with the obligations, ceremonies and celebrations that befit special circumstances, particularly with those rituals designed to confirm one's identity and those meant to atone for, cleanse from, or pacify the results of mistaken deeds and other improprieties.

The dharmasastras are "manuals" for the maintenance of dharma in one's life and community and delineate ritualistic prescriptions for reestablishing, to the degree possible, righteousness when one has wittingly or per chance gone astray. Thus, the *Laws of Manu* and similar dharma texts are blueprints for attaining and maintaining good karma in an effort to ensure an agreeable condition in the here and now as well as in future incarnations. In this sense the dharma texts provide a legalistic paradigm for what might be viewed as karmamarga.

Note that the dharma of one who acts rightly differs from person to person depending upon one's caste and one's life-stage. This is what is meant by the sanskrit term *dharmavarnashrama*, the particular duties obtaining to one of the four stages of life for a person in a particular varna. The sanskrit term *asrama* refers to these stages:

> *asrama*—refers to the four stages of spiritual effort or periods in life, i.e. 1) student; 2)householder; 3)forest dweller (hermit/renunciate); 4) sannyasi (total renunciate).

Samskara

As we noted in earlier remarks regarding karma it is with effort over many lives an individual has the potential to overcome unworthy and/or patently evil tendencies and thereby control karma. In addition to these very personal efforts, Hinduism offers other aids to facilitate a smoother spiritual and mundane life course. Among these aids are the *samskara.*

> *samskara*—Purification; refers to the ritual acts somewhat comparable to Christian sacraments; intended to protect an individual from harm; there are variously said to be 16 or 40 or more samskara to be observed during the life of an orthodox Hindu.

It is beyond the scope of this book to describe the sixteen (or forty samskaras); however, the following are among the most significant for many Hindus:

Garbhadhana—Rites to promote conception.

Jatakarma—"Birth ceremony" performed just before cutting the umbilical cord.

Namakarana—Name giving

Cudakarma—Tonsure.

Upanayana—"Second birth;" "becoming twice born;" performed for boys between eight and twelve years of age when the lad is presented to his guru (teacher); upanayana is the occasion upon which a boy from the upper three varnas is presented the *yajnopavita* (sacred thread/cord) which he will wear over his right shoulder.

Vivaha—Marriage.

Antyesti—Funeral rites.

4

Bhakti, Puja, and Sakti

Bhakti and Bhaktimarga

In this Chapter we address *bhaktimarga,* a widely popular expression and practice of the Hindu Way. Literally, the term *bhakti* means "devotion" and implies the notion of "to divide and share" (as one might with affection share food with family, friends, and those in need for example). In the spirit of bhakti, instead of attempting to apprehend an impersonal Brahman, God is perceived by the devotee as approachable and as a fountain of grace poring forth uncounted blessings that evoke within the devotee a spirit of adoration. Bhaktimarga accepts the premise that the Absolute confronts humans in a personal form in order that humans can, in turn, respond to divine grace. In bhakti, salvation is not the result of human striving but is instead a gift from God.

You may have noticed that I employed the term "God." Indeed much bhaktimarga is theistic (god-centered); therefore in this manifestation of the Hindu way , hope for moksha lies in the power of a personal God of the universe, the Absolute One who having created karma can negate it and free the devotee from samsara.

In that we can interpret Bhakti to mean "devotion" often distinguished by a range of attitudes from ecstatic rapture to obedience, it demands acts of worship via ceremonies, rituals, hymns of praise, and the veneration of statues, shrines, and holy places. But bhakti is not simple idol worship, i.e. the properly consecrated icon becomes the focus *through* which God (who cannot be represented in any image) is worshipped.

Puja

Now let's discuss a concept and ritual practice intimately connected to bhakti, i.e. *puja* :

puja—"Honor;" refers to acts of worship performed before the deity in its shrine (either at home by the eldest married male in the household or at a temple by one or several priests).

Puja is addressed to an image (idol) representing a deity. Idols are made with great ritual precision in order to entice the presence of the deity. An installation rite is performed to induce the deity to take up residence in the idol. If the deity is to remain in the idol (and that is the desired outcome) it must be given great attention e.g. baths and offerings of food and drink. Much puja is personal and not communal. Communal puja is generally associated with great festivals.

Millions of Gods?

There are numerous deities in the Hindu pantheon, and some people have speculated that more than three million deities are worshipped in India. As you recall some of the significant devas of the Vedic Period include: Agni (life force of nature; god of fire and sacrifice, messenger to the gods); Indra (sky god; god of war); Varuna (god of rita; upholder of cosmic order; has power to punish and reward); Rudra—"the Howler;" archer-god whose arrows bring disease; potentially dangerous; remote, dwelling in the mountains; guardian of healing herbs); etc.

Later in the development of the Hindu way, major devas came to include among others: Brahma (creator; lord of all creatures; above and beyond worship); Sarasvati (consort of Brahma; goddess of knowledge, learning, truth); Vishnu (preserver; controller of human fate; he draws near to mankind in ten incarnations called *avatars*; Lakshmi (wife of Vishnu; goddess of fortune and beauty; Siva (destroyer and recreator of life; source of both good and evil); Kali/Durga (consort of Siva; great mother; symbol of judgement and death).

Siva and Vishnu

You will recall that we noted that perhaps more than a million devas are the objects of various kinds of veneration in India. Among these are Siva and Vishnu both of whom are widely popular. The followers of Siva are know as *Saivas* and Vishnu's devotees are called *Vaishnavas.*

First let's turn our attention to Siva who is represented in the Vedas as Rudra (the Howler). He is a deity in whom opposites , such as creation and destruction, conjoin and then become resolved in harmony. He is often symbolized by a statue of a bull (a symbol of fertility) or as a lingam (phallus), which is symbolic of his creative nature. He is both the destroyer and creator of life (perhaps more accurately he recreates life in its endless cycle of samsara). Siva is the source of good and evil, and while he is perceived as for the "terrible one," he is also understood as perfect mildness and peaceful rest. Siva is identified with the masculine role in fertility and procreation but is often portrayed as perpetually chaste. Regarding the former he is symbolized as we have noted in the lingam (phallus) which is often "seated" in a yoni (female organ). Siva is master of yogis and is sometimes depicted half-naked, smeared with cremation ashes, skulls around his waist, and a necklace of intertwining serpents. Finally, Siva is often portrayed as king of dancers. In this representation he dances continually and thus creates, preserves, and destroys all things physical so that beings can live and learn.

Siva's wives or consorts are also powerful. They include the goddesses Uma, Parvati, and Kali/Durga. It is in connection with the goddesses Kali and Durga that we now turn to a brief view of *saktism,* often a significant part of the Saivas tradition.

saktism—A tradition wherein the divine being of Siva is thought of in female terms and where the female is the active while the male is the more passive manifestation. Saktis focus less on moksha and more on attaining and maintaining health, wealth, and other worldly goals.

Sakti is often identified with the goddess Durga who is perceived as the active power determining the course of the universe. Durga is the "One" cosmic sakti and the many other goddesses worshipped in Hinduism are seen as various forms assumed by Durga. Durga is also perceived as Kali, a dreadful and powerful manifestation of sakti. The goddess Kali is portrayed as ferocious, wearing a garland of skulls and a skirt of severed hands and seemingly paradoxically as serene. Even in her most fearful aspect, Kali is understood as granting peace to her followers by overcoming their fears; therefore, she can be and is the object of intense and passionate devotion.

Vishu is worshipped by his devotees (Vaishnavas) as the "Great Preserver." He is in charge of human fate and is a symbol of Divine love and intervention on behalf of humanity.

Some scholars believe that the Vaishnava tradition has its roots in the tribal religion of the Satvatas (5th century B.C.E.) who worshipped Krishna Vasudeva (a non-Vedic deity) who was called Bhagavat (Bounteous One). Vishnu is very popular among many Hindus. He is usually portrayed in various symbolic forms; therefore, he may be depicted for example as reclining or asleep on the ocean (which stands for chaos) or with a thousand-headed serpent who provides him with protection and symbolizes his numerous powers. He is also represented as presiding over a heavenly court, armed with a discus (representing the sun), as protector of growing plants (he protects babies in the womb), or he may be portrayed as one or more of his *avatars* performing great deeds on behalf of humanity.

avatar—One who descends; Visnu appeared on earth nine times at intervals in order to save it and to renew ancient values and destroy evil or avert disaster. The tenth incarnation is

yet to come. Krishna and Ram are the most famous avatars of Vishnu.

The avatars of Vishnu are:

1. **Matsya**—Fish; appeared at the time of the great flood to warn humankind.
2. **Kurma**—Tortoise; rescued treasures from the flood.
3. **Varaha**—Boar; raised the earth from the flood.
4. **Nara-simha**—Man-lion; defeated evil demons.
5. **Vamana**—Dwarf; defeated demons
6. **Parusha-Rama**—Rama with an axe; destroyed a kshatriya warrior caste who threatened to dominate the world.
7. **Ram-chandra**—Hero of the *Ramayana;* noble hero who combated evil in the world; the epitome of virtue
8. **Krishna**—Both avatar of Vishnu and god in his own right; Krishna is one of the most popular of the gods. He is also the hero of many myths and is depicted as lover, warrior, and king.
9. **Buddha**—"Enlightened One;" Gautama the Buddha, the founder of Buddhism.
10. **Kalki**—He is yet to come.

5

The Epics: Mahabharata & Ramayana

The *Mahabharata* is the longest poem in the world, an epic containing 100,000 verses. Not a homogeneous work, the poem is a collection of narratives. The epic's central "story line" concerns the descendents of King Bharata and the condition of ancient India where the Bharatas lived. The setting is the end of the "third age" and the great civil war which ushers in the "fourth age," the era of final disintegration and unrighteousness, i.e. the present age when the "cow of Dharma stands on one leg." In the *Mahabharata* two sets of cousins claim to be the rightful heirs to the throne of India. In the end the five Pandava brothers prevail, but only after a bitter and very long conflict. Please note that in gleaning much of the theological significance of the "story" you will need to know that the reaction of the Pandava brothers is vital, i.e. the eldest brother, Yudhishthira, hates war and wants to avoid the conflict. He seeks spiritual shelter in ascetic meditation (yoga). His third brother, Arjuna, also hates war and is deeply troubled by his conscience; however, Arjuna has great ability as a military commander and struggles mightily with his duty to his family, country, and the "good fight," versus the risk of peril to his soul as a result of the heavy negative karma that would result from killing in war.

The theological crux of the *Mahabharata* is the section entitled *Bhagavad Gita*, which for many Hindus is regarded as exceptionally sacred and is very well known among Hindus and educated persons around the world.

Now let's sum up the *Bhagavad Gita* in terms of some notable historical, literary, and theological points:

- Written approximately between the 5th and 2nd centuries B.C.E. but had existed in the oral tradition for centuries prior.

- Not originally part of the Mahabharata.

- Not sruti, but popularly regarded as especially sacred.

- The most popular "book" in Hindu religious literature and sometimes referred to as "Hindu Bible."

- Less "rational" and more mystical and emotional.

- Not concerned with Krishna as an individual but with Him as Brahman/Ultimate Reality, i.e. Krishna as the divine incarnation (avatar) of Vishnu, the god who is Arjuna's *ista deva* (chosen deity and therefore the object of his personal devotion/bhakti).

In the end, Arjuna is finally persuaded by Krishna to do battle on the basis of Krishna's arguments which are in fact divine teachings prescribing that one must do one's duty according to one's caste and that the performance of one's duty involves neither guilt nor negative karma if the duty is accomplished in a spirit of detachment., especially if the battle is waged without sentiments of hatred. Krishna teaches Arjuna that death destroys only the body and not the soul; therefore, in battle, killing results in no real harm since the soul cannot be killed. The *Bhagavad Gita* enlightens all to the realization that doing one's duty as the scriptures require and/or doing it as service to God liberates one from samsara enables one to attain moksa. In popular Hinduism this is taken by believers to promise that moksa is available to all persons without regard to caste. The promise of the *Gita* universally inclusive because Krishna instructs that knowledge, work, and devotion are all paths to moksa.

Puranas

Before we move on to the Ramayana a few words about the Cult of Gopala and the purana may be useful. The Cult of Gopala refers to the worship of Krishna in his earthly form as a cowherd boy, and the theology and practice related to the Cult are popular in India. The writings relative to the Cult are found in the Krishna cycle (a cycle of stories about Krishna) including the Bhagavad Gita; Vishnu Purana; and Harivamsa Purana.

> **purana**—**"Ancient;" devotional texts often used in Hindu bhakti cults of Vishnu; a class of writings in Sanskrit containing legendary materials describing creation, the reign of the gods, ancient kings and kingdoms; ethics; and stories relating to how the good life is to be lived, how the gods are to be worshipped, etc.**

Some additional points regarding the purana(s) are that they are:

- Widely known in one form or another by educated Hindus.

- Not considered to be scripture (certainly not sruti), but they are afforded much respectful reverence.

- Believed to have been composed by human sages in a by gone era.

- "Storehouses" of popular Hindu ideals.

- Considered by some Hindu reformers as degenerative manifestations of the ancient Vedic truth.

The Ramayana(s)

The *Ramayana* ("The Career of Rama") is one of the two great epics of the Hindu scriptures (the other being, as you know, the *Mahabharata*). Many authors do not address the fact that there is more than one version of the epic. Some of the consequences of that omission are that

much of the cultural history of India as well as a more complete understanding of the Hindu tradition are not made available to other than
subject specialists and more advanced students. In the operative Hindu
tradition there are two significant, major versions of the tale of Rama,
i.e the *Ramayana* of Valmiki and the *Ramacharita-manasa* ("The Lake
of the Acts of Rama") or the *Ramayana* of Tulasi-Dasa (Tulsi). The latter is especially popular among Hindus in North India. Thus it is significant to appreciate the essential differences in the versions and what
they mean to Hindus.

The *Ramayana* was compiled sometime in the first or second century C.E., and its authorship is ascribed to the sage Valmiki, but some
scholars hold that the tale told by Valmiki was based on either an earlier opus and/or various stories about Rama handed down through the
oral tradition. According to tradition, the author-poet Valmiki had
been a highway robber who repented and found his way into the holy
life of a forest hermit. Some accounts describe him as a contemporary
of Rama himself. Regardless of the actual facts surrounding his personal life, Valmiki is regarded as the "father" of Sanskrit poetry.

Valmiki's epic relates the biography of Rama, Prince of Ayodhya.
Rama is born as a result of a sacrifice offered by the king to the devas in
order to obtain the special boon of a son and heir to the kingdom. The
devas, troubled by Ravana, a powerful demon king, turn in desperation
to Vishnu begging him to be born in human form in order to grant the
king's petition and to rid the world of the demon. But the *Ramayana* is
more than the tale of the great God King. It is a blueprint for living a
righteous life, and some view it as a kind of extension of the dharma
literature. The epic presents myriad examples of "proper" traditional
Hindu values, norms, model relationships, etc, and it carries the message that righteousness will triumph.

Valmiki's Rama is an enormously heroic personality and the personification of moral superiority, but he is not God, at least not in Valmiki's original rendering. The divinity of Rama appears to have been
added as later interpolations. Thus, the religion of the *Ramayana* is

polytheistic. The metaphysical focus is upon dharma. Valmiki's Rama is not an object of worship but of emulation. On the other hand Tulasi's Rama is Divine, and the *Ramacharita-manasa* is the work of a devoted evangelist who created a gospel of salvation through a Blessed Lord Rama whose mercy and grace is available to all.

The author of *Ramacharita-manasa* was born into a brahman family near Rajapur in 1532 C.E. and was promptly abandoned in the belief that he was a *abhuktamula* (according to astrological indications a child destined to murder its father). According to legend the infant was found and adopted by a wandering *sadhu* (holy man) who renamed him after the sacred plant used to purify in samskara rituals. Thus he came to hold the name Tulasi-Dasa or Tulasi ("Servant of the *tulasi* plant"). The sadhu served as the boy's guru and taught him the *Ramayana*. He supposedly married, renounced the householder life, and wandered extensively in the north of India preaching about Rama. He began writing his epic in the vernacular around 1574 C.E.. Tulasi's decision to eschew the Sanskrit in favor of the lingua franca is significant. Although some have speculated that he simply lacked a command of the classical language, others have perhaps more convincingly suggested that the choice was deliberate and intended to bring the message of the sacred story closer to the people and thereby nearer to salvation.

Tulasi's intense personal devotion to Ramachandra (Rama) as an incarnation of the supreme God was central to his life, and his teaching conveyed the doctrinal principles that there is one God, that humankind's nature was inherently sinful, that the Supreme One in the form of Rama dwells in heaven from whence He is prepared to receive into salvation all who call upon Him. Infused with the vitality of Tulasi's religious beliefs, the *Ramacharita-manasa* marks the demise of Rama as a mere hero and portrays the birth and subsequent life of God. It is this *"Ramayana"* that is known to millions of Hindus and for many is less a paradigm for dharma and more a gospel of salvation in the bhakti tradition of love, adoration, mercy, and the grace of a great and personal savior. In Tulasi's poem, Rama is God and is portrayed as an utterly perfect character without a trace of human failings.

Because Tulasi's opus seems to mirror a number of significant aspects of the nature of Hinduism today, it begs our further attention. The following are a few points of comparison between the *Ramayana* and *Ramacharita-manasa.*

First, Valmiki's work begins, after a brief introduction, with a description of the setting, i.e. Ayyodya, King Dasarth's court, and his wish for a male heir. On the other hand Tulasi begins with a lengthy invocation and follows with an exhaustive description of the relationship of Siva and Sati wherein Siva is revealed as an important god, an inherent part of the *trimurti* (the three devas sometimes referred to as the "Hindu Trinity," i.e. Brahma, Vishnu, and Siva). Siva is seen as the perfect ascetic, a fountain of inexhaustable goodness through whom a devotee may reach the Supreme One.

In order to better demonstrate Rama as God, Tulasi either omits or changes Valmiki's references to Rama as weak, such as the killing of the monkey king, Bali. Tulasi also manipulates the person and character of Sita to share in Rama's divinity and reflect His divinity. Consider that in Valmiki's verses she is quite possibly raped by Ravana but in Tulasi's account it is more doubtful that such an outrage could have occurred. In the Tulasi version Rama's brother Laksman is notably more consistently devoted and there is no hint that he might desire Sita for himself. Further, in the *Ramacharita-manasa* the relationship of Rama to the other gods seems to bear witness to His status as the Supreme One, i.e. in numerous places he is worshipped by Brahma, Siva, and others.

In whatever version it may be extant, some scholars agree that the *Ramayana* may contain some historical "truth," but the "point" for us is that the epic is about: the universal and ongoing struggle between good and evil, that there is great hope for a safe passage through existence, and that righteousness will prevail.

It is useful to note that in "popular" Hinduism the Rama story is heard or seen as an enactment from childhood through old age and people know well the main characters, their history, and their nature. Hanuman, the monkey, is deified and adored especially by children.

The Rama story is a basis for everyday life in that Rama, Sita, Laksman, and others exhibit values and normative behaviors that are prescriptions for normative behavior.

6

Roots of The Dharma: Buddha Sakyamuni

A s you will recall, in the Hindu way a classic response to samsara was and continues to be renunciation. Thus the tradition of total renunciation was present in the Brahmanical religious tradition into which Saykamuni, the historical Buddha, was born in 560 B.C.E..

Religion in north India at the time of the birth of the Buddha Sakyamuni was influenced by local indigenous cults, Indus religion, Brahmanism, and various other seekers including Jains. There were numerous and diverse ascetics called *sramana(s)* living individually or collectively in *asramas* in the forests and byways of the region.

sramana(s)—"striver;" ascetic religious seekers; many sought reform of and/or opposed Brahmanism; renunciants.

The worldview of the place and time was essentially that of the Brahmanical tradition. Time was cyclical and endless, dharma determined karma, and escape from samsara, while rare, was a noble goal. As we proceed to examine the origins of Buddhism, I hope that you will be able to appreciate the "connections" between the faith, place, and cultural traditions into which Sakyamuni was born and which he ultimately altered.

Siddhartha Gautama: Buddha Sakyamuni

Overwhelmingly, serious scholars believe that the "historical" Buddha, the founder of Buddhism, actually lived, i.e. he was a historical person, and the core of Buddhism is based upon the life and teachings of Siddhartha Gautama or Sakyamuni Gautama Siddhartha. Here is what we can learn from his name: **Sakyamuni**—"Sage of the Sakyas" (is the clan name of the man);. **Gautama**—"of the lineage of Gotama" (is his surname or family name);. **Siddhartha**—"success" (is his given name). He was born in or near a village called Lumbini located in northeast India near the present border of India and Nepal in 560 B.C.E.. His family followed the way of the Brahmanical (Hindu) tradition and were members of the Ksyatria varna. Many Buddhists believe that Sakyamuni is the most recent in a series of Buddhas; therefore, Buddhism generally holds that there were Buddhas before him and there will be Buddhas to come. Indeed in the Mahayana and other streams of Buddhism, followers hold that there are numerous Buddhas in this and diverse other "dimensions." Please note that hereafter in these pages we shall refer to this Buddha as Sakyamuni. Sakyamuni was the son of Shuddhodanna who, according to tradition was the ruler of a modest "kingdom." His mother was Maya, wife of Shuddhodanna, a woman said to be a paragon of purity and who had demonstrated moral and spiritual excellence during numerous earlier incarnations. Sakyamuni himself had developed spiritually to the point of near absolute perfection over the courses of countless existences and just prior to his final incarnation dwelt in a heaven called "Tushita." It was from this high place that he chose the circumstances and time of his last birth. Sakyamuni's birth was miraculous and created a "Buddha uproar," an event accompanied by miracles, signs, and wonders. Some of the notable phenomena traditionally associated with his nativity are that: his birth followed on a vow of chastity by Maya who dreamed that a white elephant entered her womb; he was born ten months after the dream; his birth caused no pain to Maya; the earth trembled and various extrahuman beings appeared in order to pay homage; Maya died seven days after the birth (Many Buddhists hold that this was because a woman who has borne a Buddha has fulfilled her perfect destiny). Further, shortly after his birth and in accord with Brahmanical tradition, court brahmans and other holy men were summoned by the king as asked to forecast the newborn's future. They predicted that the boy would become either a *cakravartin* (universal monarch) or else a **buddha**.

buddha—"awakened one" or "enlightened one;"

According to tradition, Prince Siddhartha's father was gravely concerned that the boy would follow a spiritual path instead of the political one to which the aspired for him. Consequently, the young prince was raised under the care of his aunt and the strict supervision of his father. His upbringing was characterized by such things as: splendid luxury; careful sheltering from outside influences that might cause him to seek a spiritual path; special tutelage in the ways of a warrior, art, and practical "sciences;" the ministrations of special "dancing" girls and entertainers; and palaces. In the course of time the king arranged a marriage for him to a beautiful princess named Yasodhara who bore him a son to whom he gave the name Rahula ("chains" or "the fetter'). This somewhat unfortunate name is out of keeping with the tradition of naming a child something auspicious and some scholars believe that the name is a metaphor in the Buddha story that suggests that despite his life of luxury he felt trapped and unhappy.

Before Sakyamuni fled home for good at age 29, he made four journeys away from the palaces, and the events connected with these journeys are seminal to the Buddha story, the path his life would follow, and his teachings. According to Buddhist tradition the king, in his endeavors to shield the prince from the harsh realities of the world, ordered the streets to be cleared of such potentially troubling sights the sick, the dead, holy men, very old people, and the like whenever the prince went abroad, but despite these precautions he saw four things that caused him to finally and forever abandon the royal life and his family. What he saw on four excursions were: an elderly and frail man; a very ill person in great pain; a human corpse; and a holy man (perhaps a sannyasin or sramana). *The* prince was deeply moved and ultimately became depressed as a result of these encounters with life's realities and came to realize that life was transient and as a result what he appeared to have at the moment, his riches, his body, his family, his health, etc, would ultimately be lost to him. On the other hand, his encounter with the holy man was decisive, for the prince perceived in him an aspect of peace. The prince concluded that all life's pleasures and desires were worthless. He longed for the peace that he sensed within the heart of the holy man and for its source, i.e. "true knowledge." Thus he "escaped" the palace in the middle of the night leaving Yasodhara and Rahula asleep. He ran to the forest, got rid of his jewels, and exchanged his expensive clothes for rags.

Please recall that renunciation and flight was not entirely uncommon at the time. As we noted earlier the forests contained many sannyasis and seekers who had left ordinary society to live in spiritual communities, i.e. asramas (some of which were formed around spiritual preceptors) or as hermits. Thus, Sakyamuni began his search for "true knowledge" (the secret of liberation from samsara) in a very traditional Hindu Way: Specifically, he sought a guru, but he found no one who knew the secret of liberation. He tried yoga in a vain effort to unite his atman (self) with Brahman, but he failed. He journeyed to a place called Uruvela and followed a life of extreme self-denial in an effort to gain the threshold of moksha (he ate one grain of rice per day until his navel touched his backbone), but for all his efforts he succeeded only in ruining his health. Ultimately he came to understand that the course of extreme asceticism was useless and that he needed to be healthy in order to succeed in his quest. As Sakyamuni resumed taking appropriate nourishment and his cognitive capacities returned, he came to see, at least dimly, that what he required was insight into the very nature of reality and a change of attitude regarding greed. He became committed to seeking a Middle Way between hedonism and self-denial. Somewhere along the way of working out his deliverance he recalled a childhood experience in which he sat under an apple tree where he found both emotional comfort and clarity of mind, and it was thus that the Buddha-to-be decided to sit under a tree which was to become the **bodhi** or **bo** tree (the tree of Enlightenment), and it was within the shelter of the bodhi tree that he attained Enlightenment and became a buddha, but that glorious goal was not reached without momentous circumstances.

As he began his great meditation he was attacked by Mara (god/demon of illusion) who cast upon him hallucinations and stirred up within him feelings of ill will, anger, greed, lust and the like. The evil one dispatched a host of lesser demons to join in on the attack, but Sakyamuni stayed his course and finally reached enlightenment through the course of three nights and days. In the first stage he perceived his previous incarnations. Second, he came to understand the true nature of samsara and how it is maintained. Third, he reached a comprehension of the Four Holy Truths whereupon he became by virtue of his knowledge a fully enlightened being, a buddha.

Another term that describes a buddha is *tathagata.*

> *tathagata*—**"Perfectly enlightened one;" "one who has succeeded;" another title of the Buddha Sakyamuni.**

The Four Holy Truths

Sakyamuni's realization of the Four Holy Truths and the gnostic knowledge they contain enabled him to achieve the supreme status of a buddha, and thus he had the capacity to enter immediately into *nirvana*, but remained on earth in order to teach others the Way.

> *Nirvana*—**"Extinguish;" eternal escape from samsara; a state of freedom from all desire; release from the effects of karma; a condition of indescribable and utter peace; the normative goal of Buddhists.**

The Four Noble Truth are:

I. THE KNOWLEDGE OF SUFFERING *(duhka)*
II. THE SOURCE OF SUFFERING (tanha)
III. THE REMOVAL OF SUFFERING (niroda)
IV. THE WAY TO THE REMOVAL OF SUFFERING (marga)

The Four Noble Truths are at the core of the *Dharma* teaching.

Dharma—(Please note that the meanings of Dharma differ from the meaning in Hinduism.) First, please know that Dharma has many meanings in Buddhist texts and that the "proper" meaning of the term is determined by context and use. Depending on the context and use, Dharma can mean in Buddhism: the teachings of the Buddha; "Truth;" "Reality;" the "particles" of all things including material objects, cognitive phenomena, spiritual "matter;" and the like; furthermore as in Hinduism, Dharma may mean moral law, the "right", duty, or religion.

The Eightfold Path

The Noble Eightfold Path are teachings contained in the fourth Noble Truth, **marga**—("path leading to the end of suffering"). Herein lies much of Sakyamuni Buddha's basic teaching and the template for the holy Buddhist lifestyle. Specifically the Eightfold Path consists of the following parts:

> *Right knowledge*
> *Right attitude*
> *Right speech*
> *Right action*
> *Right living/occupation*
> *Right effort*
> *Right mindfulness*
> *Right concentration/composure*

It is beyond the scope of this book to comment further on the nature of the aspects of this teaching except to say that each of the elements of **marga** are complex, multifaceted, and rich in meaning on myriad levels of comprehension, but know that proper and efficacious understanding and implementation of each of these eight elements of the Noble Eight-Fold Path requires numerous life times of meditation, focus, and practice.

Immediately following Buddha Sakyamuni's decision to defer entering into full nirvana, he began 45 years of teaching. He traveled around in the area of the Ganges Basin and gave his first sermon at Benares. According to tradition he received as his first disciples several seekers who had once been with him but deserted him when he renounced the ascetic disciplines in favor of a middle way. Soon afterward he began to receive additional *bhikshu(s)*.

bhikshu(s)—Disciples; Buddhist sannyasi(s); monks; nuns are called *bhiksuni*.

The bhikshus and/or bhiksuni were eventually formed into the *sangha*.

sangha—Community of monks; the term may refer to either a specific monastic community, Buddhist monks and/or "nuns" in general, or those in a particular country, e.g. the Thai Sangha; the term may also describe the vinaya (monastic rules) associated with monastic life.

Among the first bhikshu were Ananda, the Buddha's cousin, and Rahula, the son of the Buddha. Buddhists believe that when the sangha grew to number about 60 bhikshu, the Sakyamu sent them out to spread Dharma. At first the sangha excluded women, but eventually the Buddha agreed to include them.

The Buddha Sakyamuni taught into old age, i.e. 80. He died of food poisoning at the town of Kushinagara. Note that Buddhist view this passing as the Buddhas's parinirvana, his entrance into "full" nirvana. His body was cremated and portions of his ashes were distributed to various places in India and possibly in other lands.

7

Development and Diffusion of Buddhism

I n the last Chapter we left the Buddha Sakyamuni in nirvana and with his earthly remains cremated and distributed. But the Dharma continued to both spread and develop. In order to appreciate how and why we will first look to the sangha and its most illustrious members, the *arhant(s).*

> *arhant/arahant*—"Worthy;" generally refers to a monk one who is deserving of reverence and offerings; one who will be released at death from samsara; a perfected saint.

A monk (or in special circumstances a layperson) who achieves the status of "arhant" is one who has through diligence in meditation and excellence in spiritual living over numerous lifetimes has overcome the barriers of greed and other barriers to nirvana. Arhants may attain nirvana upon "death" in their present lives. Thus, many Buddhists look to the sangha and its members for instruction and special "blessings." Indeed the sangha is the seat of one of **the Three Jewels** of Buddhist belief. Believers find physical and spiritual refuge as they recite: "I take shelter in the Buddha; I take shelter in the Dharma; I take shelter in the Sangha." Taking refuge in this way ensures believers that they will not be reborn in a hell or as an animal, for example.

The sangha is expected to provide the laity with models of ideal Buddhist behavior and guidance in the knowledge and practice of the Dharma. The laity are expected to know and practice the Dharma as best they can and to provide food and other requirements for the monks and/or nuns. Thus the sangha was and continues to play a major role in the transmission of Buddhism intergenerationally, cross culturally, and vast expanses of geographical space.

Originally monks and nuns wandered and lived as best they could under trees, in caves, small temporary huts, in haystacks, etc. A tradition of "forest monks" has continued until recent times in places like Thailand. The forest monks were strict in the practice of asceticism and an emphasis on yoga. Eventually most monks settled into communities. At first they settled semi-permanently only during the rainy season when travel became difficult, and then in permanent monasteries as the monastic tradition developed. Early monastic residence halls housed a *stupa*.

> *stupa*—A principal object of worship for Buddhists; stupas are especially venerated and "sacred" when they contain relics of the Buddha or else those of a revered monk.

In part as a result of the communal lifestyle associated with permanent settlements, the *vinaya* became increasingly important to ensure order, the successful operation of the monastery, and the appropriate behavior of the monks and nuns.

> *vinaya*—rules for monastic life; in addition to delineating procedures for rituals and the like, it also prescribes guidelines for conflict resolution; the vinaya may differ from community to community but contains universal elements that apply everywhere, e.g. prohibitions against killing, stealing, lying, sexual misconduct, and the consumption of alcohol.

The rule also requires that members of the sangha be celibate and renounce material goods.

Now let's turn to the second of the Three Jewels, the Dharma. Please note that normative Therevada Buddhist belief does not center on the veneration of Buddha Sakyamuni, but operatively much Buddhist practice includes such veneration. The latter is often cause for confusion among outside observers and Buddhists alike. Most Buddhists in countries where Therevada Buddhism prevails worship in one way or another the Buddha and petition him for interventions and boons of all kinds, but in "theory" for Therevadists, Sakyamui Buddha is not a deity, nor a mediator or "savior." Indeed, he cautions his disciples not to seek his ministrations after he entered into nirvna because he could not respond from that state. Thus in Buddhism it is the Dharma that takes precedence over the Buddha, for it is the Dharma that enables one to do what no one else can do for one, i.e. obtain the blessed release of nirvana. For the moment let's think of the Dharma as "knowledge." In Buddhism the kind of knowledge inherent in the Dharma is different from what we in the West may think of as knowledge. As we noted in the previous Chapter the core of Buddhist knowledge lies in the Four Noble Truths and the Eightfold Path. Essential, too, to Dharma knowledge is *pratitya-samutpada*. A full discussion of this concept is beyond the scope of this book, but for our purposes we may note that it translated as "dependent origination," "dependent co-arising," "conditioned arising," or "interdependent arising." It may be helpful to view pratitya-samutpada as the Buddhist "law of cause and effect" because it is a model for comprehending the nature of suffering and why beings are ensnared in samsara. It is by meditating upon pratitya-samutpada that Buddhists may come to share in Sakyamuni's awakening to the realization that "self" is a fiction caused by ignorance and which leads to suffering. Thus Buddhism holds to the doctrine of *anatman*.

> *anatman*—"no self;' the belief that there is no inherently existing self, and that the one who perceives this truth will no longer cling to an imaginary "I" which is a main cause of suffering.

Perhaps it might be helpful if we pause a moment to address the notion held by some observers that Buddhism is pessimistic, especially in that it seems to teach that life is suffering. The Pali Canon (the corpus of Buddhist teachings first written down in the Pali language during the first century B.C.E. in Sri Lanka) and other early textual sources describe the historical Buddha and his followers as calm, cheerful, and humorous. Indeed, as one who has socialized with Buddhist monks and observed them within and outside of temple or monastic precincts, I can report without hesitation that generally members of the sangha appear to have carried on in that vein. Further, after three years of residence in a Buddhist society (Thailand), I say without hesitation that my most devout Buddhist friends and acquaintances are a life affirming and fun loving lot, indeed.

The notion that Buddhism is in fact life affirming is evidenced in the doctrine of *ahimsa*.

ahimsa—Noninjury/nonviolence to living things.

In general, the doctrine of ahimsa is shared by Hindus, Jains, and Buddhists, but these religions have somewhat different interpretations of and operative approaches to ahimsa that are beyond the scope of our present studies; therefore, for our purposes in gleaning an understanding of Buddhism and its cultural contexts let's examine how ahimsa was understood and practiced in early Buddhism under the great Mauryan monarch, Asoka.

Asoka

King Asoka (264–227 B.C.E.) was a great conqueror and Buddhist king. His devotion led him, in the pursuit of ahimsa, to ban royal hunting parties and replace them with religious pursuits, e.g. pilgrimages. Although Asoka was a vegetarian, in general Buddhists are not, and while monks, nuns, and other particularly devout believers adhere closely to ahimsa, most Buddhist follow the practice to the degree practicable in the course of their various lives and vocations. Asoka reigned as Emperor of the Mauryan Empire from approximately 268–232 B.C.E.. During his reign the empire extended over vast areas of India. Until the early 20th century Western scholars viewed him as a legendary figure, but in 1837 certain inscriptions were deciphered for the first time and other archaeological evidence was uncovered that revealed that the great king was a historical person, and eventually scholars acknowledged the fact of his existence.

What we know about Asoka is mostly gleaned from Buddhist writings and the so-called "edicts," i.e. 14 edicts engraved on rocks (the "rock edicts") and 7 edicts inscribed on stone pillars. From these sources we know that he: was an intensely devout Buddhist; established what was to become a model Buddhist political state; played a highly significant role in propagating Buddhism (he is sometimes referred to as a "Second Buddha"); was dedicated to the doctrine of ahimsa and ultimately became a pacifist; was dedicated to the welfare of humanity and other sentient creatures, including animals. during his reign and perhaps his patronage, Buddhist monks traveled from India to the Greek States spreading the faith. Buddhist sources relate that during these years 73,000 converts were made, 1,000 monks ordained, and 84,000 stupas were built.

Asoka did not begin his reign as either a pacifist or pious Buddhist. Buddhist sources relate that he assumed the throne by killing off his rivals (he reportedly murdered 99 male relatives and 500 high officials). He began his political career as a tyrant (he was known as "Asoka the Tyrant). In the seventh year of his reign he became a Buddhist studied the Dharma, lived among monks as a lay brother, and gave up hunting; however, shortly thereafter he went to war against a neighboring state. The ensuing conflict resulted in 100,000 enemy deaths and the capture 150,000. Because of the loss of life Asoka became deeply moved with grief and guilt. He vowed never to wage war again and proclaimed a new policy of "Peaceful Dharma Conquest." As a result he became known as "Asoka of the Dharma."

As Asoka of the Dharma, the king: declared that all humans were his children; forbid animal sacrifice and restricted the use of animals as food; maintained but took steps to make the death penalty more humane; instituted the provision of social services and other humane facilities for citizens and sojourners alike, e.g. fruit trees were planted along highways to provide free food and shade, wells were dug and rest houses built, medicinal plants were cultivated and made available, etc.

Early Great Councils and Schism

According to Buddhist tradition, following the parinirvana of Buddha Sakyamuni his followers gathered together in a convention attended by about 500 arahats. This gathering is referred to as "The First Council." It was here that two collections of teachings were recited (they were transmitted via an oral tradition as it was not until much later that they were committed to writing). The two collections were the *sutra pitaka* ("basket" of discourses) and *vinaya* (regulations/rule for the monastic life which we discussed earlier).

sutra— "Thread;" discourses (teachings) of the Buddha.

BuddhBuddhist sacred writings are generally classified in terms of *pitaka*.

Pitaka— "Basket;" the earliest writings were made on leaves which were tied together and kept in a basket(s); pitaka may refer to a collection of sutra or other writings.

In the Buddhist tradition the word *tripitaka* is employed to describe three categories of Buddhist sacred writings.

tripitaka—"Triple basket;" core or Buddhist scriptures; the three categories of writings within the tripitaka are generally understood to be:

1. vinaya—"basket of discipline;" rules for monastic livings; monastic regulations; history of the sangha
2. sutta-pitaka—"basket of discourses"
3. abhidharma—scholastic works

Thus the First Council served to "codify" and preserve what many Buddhists hold are the teachings of Buddha Sakyamuni himself.

The Second Council was held at Vaisali sometime between 330 and 350 B.C.E. (or approximately 100 years after the death of the historical Buddha). For our purposes, the principal significance of the Second Council is that it resulted in the Mahasanghika (great assembly or majority) Schism (sometimes called the "basic schism"). (Please note that I am not suggesting that the Second Council specifically created the division between Therevada and Mahayana, a division that was long in the making and is attributable to several factors, but The Second Council does, I think, enable us to distinguish the emergence of Therevada as a distinct tradition and have a somewhat clearer perspective on some of the roots of Mahayana.) The historical details regarding the Second Council differ depending on whose accounts one consults. The Therevada version suggests that the elders, i.e. the arhant monks Yasa and Revata, called for the assembly in order to charge that the vinaya was being violated, e.g. monks were lacking in discipline, accepting money, in lieu of food, eating after noon, etc. According to the version(s) offered by theMahayana tradition, a monk named Mahadeva initiated the Second Council and raised five criticisms against the dominant arahants. Mahadeva charged that the arahants had failed to overcome their sexual desires, lacked omniscience (as evidenced by their need to ask directions while travelling), had spiritual doubts, and other shortcomings that spoke to their failure to live up to their claims of nearly perfected beings. In seeking to untangle the issues I find it useful to appreciate some of the undercurrents in the background of the debate. One of the issues was the spiritual status of the laity, i.e. could a lay person achieve the status of arhant? By the time of the Second Council arhant monks were the ruling elite of the sangha and for various reasons they had come as a class to alienate other monks and laypersons as well. Only monks were recognized as arhant, and they clung to that lofty status in part by holding firm to the claim that they alone knew the true Dharma. The arhant monks held that they had the right to adjudicate on the opinions and spiritual worthiness of others. The proceedings o the Second Council resulted in rejection the authority of the arhant by the majority and was manifest in the basic schism. Between 200 B.C.E. and 500 C.E. Buddhism emerged in at least two distinct "streams" (Therevada and Mahayana) with each claiming to offer the authentic Dharma.

8

Therevada and Mahayana Buddhism

Therevada

First please allow me to attempt to offer a caveat from the point of view of one who has been for several years "in the field" in Southeast Asia. Specifically, Buddhism as I have and will continue to describe it in this book, manifests itself quite differently in operative practice. That is to say that, for instance, while Therevada is doctrinally non-theistic, in practice it is often overwhelmingly theistic, inextricably interwoven with indigenous beliefs such as animism, interconnected with magic, and otherwise syncretistic within the belief systems inherent in the diverse cultural contexts in which it is found. This point may be further illustrated briefly by the idea of the stupa. Stupa(s) as you recall are memorial mounds; originally built India to receive portions of the Buddha's relics. As you will further recall, early Buddhists met together and honored the Buddha Sakyamuni in caves and around his reliquary stupas until sometime around the beginning of the first century C.E. when the Buddha began to be worshipped in the form of images. Stupas, however, followed the spread of Buddhism, and these structures came to contain relics of monks who were believed to have special powers and became themselves objects of worship. In places like Thailand, Burma , Laos, etc, some monks now traffic in magical and mantic practices. The result of these and numerous other variables is that popular Therevada in practice belies what we learn in some textbooks and in much Buddhist exegesis. A way to reconcile this dissonance is through understanding and employing the conceptual models of "ideal" versus "real" dimensions of culture. Specifically, ideal culture refers to values and norms the people in a society will profess to hold and practice while the real cultural dimension presents a people's actual practices. Some anthropologists, including myself, prefer to employ the concepts of **normative** versus **operative** to describe the lack of congruence between what people say they believe and do and what they **actually** say and do. For example, according to **normative** Therevada Buddhism it is pointless to pray to Buddha Sakyamuni because he is in nirvana, but as my field observations clearly confirm, Therevada Buddhists as a matter of course pray to him with great regularity, and this practice is a characteristic of **operative** Therevada

> *Therevada*—**"Tradition or teachings of the elders;" sometimes inappropriately called "hinayana," a descriptor which many Therevada Buddhist find offensive and inaccurate; Therevadins hold that they adhere to Buddha Sakyamuni's original teachings; the tradition emphasizes individual effort toward the attainment of spiritual progress and nirvana.**

Generally, Therevada Buddhists believe that nirvana can be achieved only by monks and, further, that this perfect attainment is nearly impossible even for illustrious members of the sangha; therefore, Therevada is viewed as "the small vehicle," a way by which only a few will reach nirvana. Both normatively and operatively Therevadins believe that most practitioners can at best hope for a favorable rebirth rather than nirvana. Normatively, Therevada: is, as we noted earlier, nontheistic, e.g. insisting that the Buddha Sakyamuni is not a deity; the locus of spiritual efficacy is in the Dharma not in any person or extrahuman entity; emphasizes meditation; recognizes up to as many as 28 Buddhas with Sakyamuni being the most recent and lookd to the coming of Buddha Maitreya who is to come; etc.

Mahayana

As you recall The Second Council marked a major schism within early Buddhism. In time the Mahasanghikas developed their teachings and perhaps incorporated them with other schools. Sometime between 100 B.C.E–100 C.E. these collective teachings began to be known as Mahayana

> *Mahayana*—"Large vehicle;" holds that nirvana is intended for all; is characterized by its soteriological nature, e.g. the bodhisattvas and Buddhas whose "saving" nature of compassion brings others to heavens and nirvana.

As we noted in the above, central to Mahayana is the belief that nirvana is not exclusively intended for just a few people. All people have within them a Buddha nature and the potential for salvation. Mahayana offers a wide path capable of leading all to ultimate bliss. Mahyanists believe in a virtually infinite number of Buddhas, Buddhas in the making, and Buddas to come, all of whom may be reached via meditation and/or prayer. The place of Sakyamuni Buddha is important but not central in the belief system.

An especially distinguishing characteristic of Mahayana Buddhism is the *bodhisattva(s)*.

> *bodhisattva*—a "saint" or semi-divine being who has renounced or postponed entrance into nirvana in order to help others to salvation/deliverance; in Mahayana Buddhism bodhisattvas are venerated as symbols of compassion and/or are called upon as saviors; bodhisattvas can "absorb" others into their own essences and carry the "absorbed" ones onward either to heaven or nirvana.

Whether manifest as human beings or celestial extrahumans, bodhisattvas are ultimately destined for enlightenment and/or Buddhahood. Bodhisattvas take vows to save as many other people as possible and promise to continue unflaggingly to carry on their missions in each of their future incarnations. As supreme paragons of compassion (perhaps the greatest virtue in the spiritual ife of a Mayahanist), bodhisattvas assist devotees in mundane matters as well as in the realms of the sacred.

According to early Mahayana doctrine (100 C.E.–300 C.E.), there are ten bodhisattva stages (*bhumi*), and it takes at least three eons for a bodhisattva to pass through these developmental stages from a beginner to a great savior. Mahayanists believe that the bodhisattva path begins with *bodhicitta*.

bodhicitta—**Thought of or desire for enlightenment" and the commencement of eternal compassion for helping others; perhaps more easily understood in Western terms as a profound "conversion experience.**

Now let's turn briefly to the Mahayana scriptures, Celestials, and heavens. Mahayana accepts the basic writings of Therevada plus numerous additional texts called *sutra* (in the Pali "*sutta*'). Indeed this stream of Buddhism has many branches and each of these has a scriptural tradition of its own. It is interesting to note that some Mahayana branches claim that their sutra(s) originate with Sakyamuni or are older still. In view of the fact that Mahayana is more recent than Therevada, some Mahayanist claim that their sutras had been preserved and hidden from human eyes by mythological serpent spirits who kept them in underwater caves until the world was ready to receive the special knowledge contained within them. Some Mahayanists hold that whatever an enlightened disciple (e.g. a bodhisattva) teaches is to be taken as the Buddha Sakyamuni's (or else one of the many other Buddha's) own teaching. As we noted earlier, the Mahayana pantheon contains numerous personages/entities whom may be worshipped, venerated, and/or propitiated. Among these are the Celestial Bodhisattvas and Celestial Buddhas; therefore, Mahayana offers, depending on the tradition, alternatives to nirvana (e.g. heavens of various kinds). One of these is Sukhavati ("happiness having" or "Paradise of the West").

Sukhavati was created by Amitabha, a Celestial Buddha. Sukhavti, like other "heavens" in Mahayana, is a place of happiness where all obstacles to the attainment of nirvana are removed. Sukhavati heaven is for many believers an end in itself where they may live happily indefinitely.

Although India and its religious traditions provided the seminary, cradle, and springboard for Buddhism, today fewer than two percent of Indians are Buddhists. The causes for its virtual disappearance in the land of its birth include the persistence of the Hindu tradition, the conquests of Muslim invaders, and the appeal of Islam.

9
Sikhism

Introductory Note

Please know that you will find that in this book I approach and treat the subject of the Sikh religion somewhat differently in terms of both the approach and style with which I have addressed the other religious traditions discussed in these pages. This is so for several reason, the foremost being that in 1974 I was awarded a Shell International Fellowship to conduct field research among the Akali Sikhs in Bangkok, Thailand. At that time, I was a doctoral candidate in anthropology at Syracuse University where I was privileged to study with Professor H. Daniel Smith of the Department of Religion, Drs. Susan Wadley and Barton Schwartz, and the renowned Swami Agehananda Bharati in the Department of Anthropology, but my teachers also included Ms. Uma Sharma and Mr. Gurnek Singh who were on the staff of the Bird Library. These fine scholars taught me among many other invaluable lessons the worth of good observation, analysis, and especially the value of the special insights gleaned from participant observation and the emic approach. Thus, over the years I have found that my students have both benefited from and enjoyed learning through sharing my field notes, collected materials, and anecdotes; therefore, I share some of these in this Chapter.

Nanak the Founder

Sikhism was founded by Guru Nanak who was born in 1469 C.E. in the Punjab region (Northwest India and Eastern Pakistan) in a town that is now located in present day Pakistan. Note that the title "Guru" is highly significant in the Sikh tradition and that we shall focus upon it in some detail later. Nanak was born a Hindu, probably a lower caste ksatryia. According to tradition he studied Sanskcrit, and Arabic, and Persian under a village Brahman and perhaps continued his studies in a religious school. In the somewhat heterogeneous multicultural context of his upbringing, he probably gleaned a basic knowledge of both Hinduism and Islam. Tradition also informs us that he had close Muslim as well as Hindu friends and associates, "soul mates" who shared his religious zeal and with whom he worshipped. At age 13 at his *upanayana* ceremony (investiture with the sacred thread) he shocked and scandalized his family by refusing investiture (as you recall this *samskara* is a fundamental ritual in the sacramental life cycle of the "twice born" Hindu male). This event is interpreted in various ways by believers many of whom hold that the boy who was to become Baba Nanak, Guru, taught in this courageous act that caste exclusivity and the Sacred were not compatible in God's ultimate plan. In due time he renamed himself Nanak, "Belonging to the Lord." Sikh tradition relates a number of unusual events and trance states that surround his early life, but a singular transformational experience for Nanak was related to an incident that occurred when he was 30 years old. He was bathing at a river, went into a trance, and disappeared for three days. He then reappeared mysteriously at the same spot. Declaring that he had been at God's throne where he had been given a mission, he gave away all his possessions and began to teach that **"There is no Hindu nor Muslim."**

Diverse Sikh traditions teach numerous claims regarding Nanak including that: he traveled to Mecca and to Tibet; performed various miracles; and converted masses of people. On the other hand some Sikhs and outsiders argue that Nanak denounced miracles but uplifted the status of women and, while not abolishing caste, he held it in disdain. Significant to Sikh cultus and their sense of identity as a "people," Nanak instituted the use of the vernacular (the Gurmuki/Punjabi language) in worship (indeed Sikhism is intimately interconnected with the peoples and subcultures of the Punjab region of Northwestern South Asia, i.e. Pakistan and Northwest India many of whom are Punjabi speakers).

Japji: Nanak's Revelations

Guru Nanak taught his followers about God in terms of that which was revealed to him and in accordance with his perceptions. Nanak was a monotheist and taught that God is formless, omnipresent, and known through His grace via the nature of "guru." Nanak's divine insight is captured in the *Japji*, a lengthy prayer offered daily (usually around dawn) by many Sikhs. [The selections that follow in this Chapter are from a volume of the prayer presented to me by members of the Sri Guru Singh Sabha in Bangkok, Thailand. The volume, *Sri Japji of Sri Guru Nanak Devji* (S. Gurbakash Singh [ed.], Bombay: The Veekay Weekly, 1974) presents the prayer in Punjabi and English.]

The opening verses reveal Nanak's understanding of the Supreme Being, i.e.:

> *God is One*
> *He has form none*
> *He is O'nkaar, the Word ever abiding*
> *His Name is [sat] everliving*
> *He's Creator and Manindwelling*
> *Fearless, enmity free*
> *Immortal Being is He*
> *He takes not birth*
> *Ever exists by Himself*
> *His Light is of His Own*
> *By Grace of Guru, God is known. (p.2)*

The *Japji* contains numerous elements of Nank's teachings. The Guru reveals that God cannot be reached via various traditional Hindu ways, e.g. ritual cleansing, yoga meditation, intellectual means, nor ascetic practices:

> *By cleansing body, if we wash it for*
> *Hundredthousand times, purity of mind results not.*
> *Even if 'avowed silence,' I should observe*
> *And without cease or stop do keep reserve*
> *Mind settles not in His thought*
> *If from food taking we abstain*
> *And so world loads of wealth obtain*
> *Hunger of mind appeases not.*
> *Mere intellectual exercises to attain Him*
> *Thousands, hundredthousands of them,*
> *Being ego based, shall all fall short*
> *Not one would help us to realise God. (p.2)*

All things are ordained by God's will and salvation is given graciously to anyone through His name:

> *By Ordainment are creatures created...*
> *By Ordainment some beget His Grace*
> *By Ordainment some ever transmigrate...*
> *God is Eternal, He is of abiding Name...*
> *They beg of Him "Lord did I bestow!"*
> *And the Benevolent One grants them so...*
> *And what words shall then from our lips flow*
> *Hearing which to us, He would His Love bestow?*
> *'Ambrosial predawn hours' is offering to male*
> *Dwell on True Name, His praises contemplate...*
> *His Grace alone leads to the Salvation Door. (pp. 4–6)*

The *Japji* provides evidence that Nanak's teachings are formulated around a monotheistic synthesis, a position that is troublesome for both fundamentalist Sikhs and scholars, i.e. there is some debate over whether Sikhism is an independent religion or a syncretism, an amalgamation of Hinduism and Islam. That argument is beyond the scope of this work, but because of its interest to some students and, scholars I have included a discussion of some dimensions of the question in a paper appended to this book ("An Observation On Macauliffe's *The Sikh Tradition*: The Teachings of Guru Nanak In A Traditional Hindu Idiomatic Paradigm?") Here, too, the *Japji* provides us with some insight into the nature of this monotheistic synthesis:

> *In the Guru I divine Siva, the Destroyer*
> *In the Guru I find Vishnu, the Sustainer*
> *In the Guru I cognise [sic] Brahma, the Creator*
> *In the Guru I see consorts of the Trinity*
> *The goddess trio: Parvati, Lakshami and Sarswati...*
> *Hearkening to Name, does mystic ascetics make*
> *Muslim Pirs, Master Yogies and sages great. (pp. 8–12)*

Thus far we have seen Nanak refer to the Supreme One variously as "God," "Guru;" and "Name (*nam*.") Following on Nanak and others in Sikhism God is called "Truth." Let's consider what these descriptors mean to believers.

Guru—"Teacher;" spiritual preceptor; in Sikhism the term refers to God, the essence of the ten gurus, and/or to the Holy Scripture(s), i.e. *Granth (Adi Granth* and/or *Guru Granth Sahib).*

Nam—"Name of God;" represents the path to God; the essence of revelation and salvation.

Sat—"Truth;" a principal aspect of the essential nature of God; God is Truth.

Holding that an emic approach may be instructive in accessing operative aspects of Sikhism, I offer the following from another publication [G. S. Sidhu, *Introduction to Sikhism*, Gravesend, U.K: The Sikh Missionary Society, 1973] provided by my informants at the Sri Guru Singh Sabha in Bangkok (please note that the Singh Sabha does not universally represent Sikhism nor does the referenced publication, but both the Singh Sabha and The Sikh Missionary Society do echo the voices of a significant number of Sikhs worldwide and is on that basis worth considering; however, by way of caveat please know that The Singh Sabha is a Sikh reform movement begun in the 1870's and which had/has among its objectives the advent of a renascence in Sikh religion and to protect it from inroads of Hinduism and Christianity):

> *According to Sikhism the very first and primal definition of God is Truth. He is eternal, infinite and omnipresent. He is the creator and is free from birth and death. He can be realised by acting upon the advice of the true Guru, who offers the devotee the wealth of true name instead of asking him to praise the Guru. He has no special temple and has no chosen people. His gifts and are showered equally aaon all. His abode is the heart of each living person and He resides on the lips of the saints who sing nothing but his praises. He is love and expects the whole creation to act in His own love. (p.31)*

Neither Nanak nor the nine Gurus who followed him claimed to be God per se. Most Sikhs believe that "God speaks to the devotees through the Guru and arouses their souls to true spiritual effort"(Ibid. p. 33). Instead Sikhism normatively holds that "Men of God like Guru Nank are so near to the Lord that there is not much difference between the Lord and His messengers...[But] To say that any religious messenger was God is heresy (Ibid. p. 34).

The Gurus

Fundamental to an appreciation of mainstream Sikhism is at least a passing acquaintance with its Gurus. The ten Gurus are:

I. Nanak (1469–1539)
II. Angad (1504–1552)
III. Amar Das (1479–1574)
IV. Ram Das (1534–1581)
V. Arjan (1563–1606)

VI. Har Gobind (1595–1644)
VII. Har Rai ((1631–1661)
VIII. Har Krishan (1656–1664)
IX. Teg Bahadur (1621–1675)
X. Gobind Singh (1666–1708)

Sikh doctrine and practice continued to develop, and, indeed, certain dramatic changes occurred under some of the ten Gurus. We will look at these shortly. For the time being let's get an overview of some terms and concepts that emerged as Sikhism developed. First let's focus briefly on the term "Sikh."

Sikh—"Disciple;" essentially the term describes one who follows the way of Sikhism, but because of sectarian and other differences not all Sikhs are agree on what Sikhism means nor upon whom may be considered a Sikh.

In general Sikhs believe in accordance with the teachings of the Gurus and scripture that God is the True Guru (*satguru*) whose *shabad* is revealed via the Gurus:

Shabad—Divine word; revealed truth; gnostic knowledge.

Shabad is conveyed through the Guru's whom some Sikhs appear to perceive as incarnations of one another. Thus the Guru can mean in Sikhism the ten Gurus collectively. Here is how it is expressed by G.S. Sidhu:

> *Today the Gurus are not amongst us in human form but their word is making them relive as such. The Guru's mind is open to us through the word and that is why the last of the Gurus declared that after him the faithful will call the Holy Book their Guru. Those who want to see the Guru are asked to read, understand and act upon the Guru's word contained in the Holy Granth. (Ibid. p. 34)*

Thus the Guru is manifest in the *Granth*.

:

Adi Granth /Guru Granth Sahib—The Sacred Book (Scriptures) of the Sikhs; as *Guru Granth Sahib* the book is the "living" presence of the Guru.

Dasam Granth—A book of "scripture" believed by some Sikhs to have been written by the Tenth Guru, Gobind Singh; it is discussed later and addressed in detain in a paper (*Guru Gobind Singh: Son of God, Avatar, or Guru?"*) appended to this book.

The sacred scriptures are believed to be the Guru, and thus they are venerated. Perhaps the following observations will help to make this point more clear. During my tenure as a guest and visiting scholar at the Gurdwara Siri Guru Singh Sabha in Bangkok, I was on several occasions privileged to visit the terraced rooftop rooms of the temple where the Holy Book was kept in repose during the times it was not installed in the public worship hall. These precincts were made fragrant with fresh flower petals and perfume. The *Granth* was maintained on a raised platform and covered in fine cloths sprinkled with flowers. My hosts explained that it was here that the *Guru Granth Sahib* was gently awakened before dawn, "bathed" by sprinkling of fragrant waters, offered nourishment, and received veneration and prayer. Afterwards the *Granth* was reverently removed to the worship hall. Similar ministrations were rendered when the *Granth* was lodged for the night rest. My hosts informed me that during World War II an aircraft dropped a bomb that landed on the temple and lodged unexploded directly adjacent to the Holy Book. Fearing for the Guru several members of the congregation risked their lives to dislodge and carry the bomb away. The *Granth* is a living Being, it is Guru, *nam, sat,* and *shabad.*

The Gurus After Nanak

Guru Angad became Guru following the death of Nanak in 1539. He was a Hindu, probably of a lower caste, and according to some Sikh traditions he was personally converted by Nanak, who, finding his own sons unworthy, chose Angad to succeed him. Angad is believed to have composed some prayers, but his principal contribution to the Faith may have been his zeal for preaching and teaching in the vernacular, i.e. Punjabi.

Guru Amar Das like Angad was also born a lower caste Hindu and was a Vaishnavite until his conversion by Angad. Amar Das: established 22 *manjis* (missionary centers); oversaw the compilation of the former Gurus' teachings; and according to some traditions he ordered a ban on *purdah* (covering of womens' faces) and *sati* (ritual burning to death of widows). Amar Das also institutionalized the *langar*.

Langar—Free kitchen; Sikh temple complexes include a "soup" kitchen where all are welcome for meals and fellowship; the langar signifies the egalitarian ideals and doctrines of the Faith.

Guru Ram Das became Guru upon the death of Amar Das in 1574 and was the first Guru born a Sikh. His origins were humble. As a boy he came to serve Amar Das whose daughter he married. Amar Das chose him as his successor over his own sons. As a spiritual master he wrote poetic verses, but he also had a keen appreciation of the role of commerce. In addition to encouraging Sikhs to become businessmen, he founded the present city of Amritsar where he ordered to be excavated the sacred pool around which the Golden Temple was to founded (we shall focus in some length on this Gurdwara later). In order to better appreciate Ram Das' gambit, it may be useful to know that Amritsar was built on a significant trade route and soon prospered the Sikhs while providing a fulcrum for and facilitated the funds for the propagation of the Faith.

Guru Arjan, the youngest son of Ram Das, was named Guru in 1581 and thus became the first to inherit the status of Guru. Arjan's contributions to the development of the religion were significant especially in that he: oversaw the composition of the *Adi Granth*, ordered the construction of the first gurdwara at the site that was later to become the Harimandir Sahib (known outside of Sikhism as the "Golden Temple"), and was the composer of numerous sacred hymns.

He also instituted a system of revenue collection (*masand*), and institutionalized doctrinal proscriptions against: pilgrimages (except to Amritsar), wearing the sacred thread, caste, asceticism, and other vestiges of Hinduism and Islam. Guru Arjan was the first Sikh Guru to be martyred as a result of his increasing stance against Muslim aggression. His martyrdom in 1606 marks a turning point in the history of the Sikhs and the development of Sikhism became increasingly characterized by a militant transformation under **Guru Hargobind** who was 11 years old when he became Guru.

Trained in martial arts by those in his inner circle and perhaps deeply affected by the murder of his father, Hargobind sought to fortify and arm the Sikhs. Indeed he did battle with numerous Moghul forces but perhaps as a result of exhaustion and/or piety he withdrew from his military operations and elected to spend the final ten years of his life in meditation.

Guru Har Rai became Guru in 1644. He lived an essentially quiet life out of the sight of the Muslim authorities. He died in 1661 and was succeeded by **Guru Har Krishan** who was five years old. The child Guru died three years later from small pox and was succeeded by his uncle, **Tegh Bahadur.**

Guru Tegh Bahadur was challenged and harassed by various "pretenders" to the title and was eventually even denied access to the Golden Temple. Despite internal and external resistance from both Sikhs and Muslims his leadership was instrumental in converting large numbers to Sikhism. the Muslim ruler, Auranzeb, arrested the Guru at Agra and had him beheaded in 1675.

The tenth Guru was the renowned warrior **Guru Gobind Singh** who brought about radical and enduring changes to Sikhism. Born in 1666 this son of son of Tegh Bahadur became Guru at the age of nine. A child prodigy, he became a prolific contributor to the *Dasam Granth* which he composed with the assistance of 52 collaborators. My own reading of the Sikhscriptures and exegesis seems to confirm what some other scholars have observed, i.e. Gobind Singh linked himself and his spiritual and temporal authority with the Hindu deity Rama, avatar of Vishnu (see the appendix for an in depth treatment of this issue in the paper "Guru Gobind Singh: Son of the Sword"). The Tenth Guru described his mission on earth as a military one and introduced the doctrine of *dharma yudh* (battle for the survival of righteousness). The following are some of the principal doctrines and dogmas instituted by the Guru:

- God was presented as *Dusht Daman* (Sword and Avenger).

- The institution of the Guru as a living man was discontinued and replaced with the *Adi Granth* and the *Khalsa Panth* (the community of Sikhs).

- *amrit* ("baptism or initiation") was institutionalized; NB: Amrit is also a "sacramental" food taken in the gurdwara as part of certain worship services.

- Sikhs were to be known/called **Singh** (Lion).

With regard to the latter, a "Sikh Catechism" (*Sri Kirtan Sohila Sahib: The Bed Time Sikh Prayer*, Amritsar: The Veekay Weekly, [1974]) provided by my informants in Bangkok, offers the following explanation of a Singh:

> *An alround* [sic] *man of lioness heart who offers his life to Guru and God. This fraternity was baptised with Nectar* [amrit] *first when five offered heads to Master, Tenth Sri Guru Gobind Singh Ji, who created Khalsa, the Pure the Saint—Soldier, the Saint-farmer, the Saint-worker who did everything wordly dutifully religiously lived life exhuberantly, happily, magnanimously yet at heart who did belong only to God ever busy serving humanity with no selfish thought ever willing to sacrifice for HIM and woo Death*
> *—god. Khalsa belongs to the Wonderous God and with God, victory is Khalsa's prennial lot...He makes an honest living and with others, he's always sharing at heart always to God attaching and day and night His name saying. He bows to none but Guru and God Wedded*

to truth, fearless doth walk Frightens none and never gives to boasting For belongs to God, he and all his belonging. (p.21).

Perhaps of special significance in terms of the development of Sikh tradition and its posture as a fierce warrior arm of God, Guru Gobind Singh instituted the *panj kakke* or five cultic manifestations ("Five Ks") or symbols that distinguish Khalsa Sikhs, i.e.:

- **kesh**(uncut hair)

- **kangha** (comb)

- **kachha**(short pants)

- **kara** (steel bangle/bracelet)

- **kirpan** (sword/dagger)

When instituted by the Tenth Guru the Five Ks were symbols of "baptism" or initiation into the **Khalsa** ("Brotherhood of the Pure"). Normatively within the context of modern day Sikhism they serve to distinguish an individual as a Khalsa Sikh and symbolize: (kachha) chastity, readiness for military action, and agility; (kara) God/Guru as *Maha Lob* "Great Steel" and as "Holy Sword," the ideals of Sikh behavior; (kirpan) "sword" or dagger, usually a very small symbolic replica carried by Khalsa Sikhs or perhaps wrapped in the folds of the turban, a symbol of defense, God, or freedom; (kesh) uncut hair worn in the manner of the ancient holy saints/seers in order to worn to remind Sikhs of their obligation to model their lives after the saints; (kangha) a symbol of cleanliness and therefore health and strength.

Following the death of Guru Gobind Singh in 1708, Sikhism suffered from political and religious disintegration, Hinduization, sectarianism and conflict until it was reorganized and strengthened under Maharaja Ranjit Singh (1780–1839). In the 1870's Sikhism began to show signs of Westernization and Modernization. In the 1920's the Sikh Gurdwara Reform Movement and the emergence of the Akali Dal helped to shape orthodox Sikhism in the 20th century.

Significant Doctrines and Practices

As monotheists Sikhs believe that God created the world and made Himself known in the whole of creation. Thus creation itself enables us to understand something of the power and will of God, and it is through the power of Divine Grace that sincere devotees are able to experience Him through worship and meditation. Sikhism holds that as devotees become increasingly aware of God they will consequently come to understand that they are encapsulated in selfishness, pleasure seeking, pride, and other wrongful inclinations that separate them from salvation and that their sole hope is the True Guru who will unite them with Himself.

Community looms large in Sikhism, and believers are enjoined to become members of active congregations where they are to worship, focus upon Sat Guru, and offer hymns of praise.

Sikhism teaches that human beings are inherently flawed because the are under the power of *haumain.*/*manmat:*

Haumain—self-centered pride.

Manmat—egosim.

Believers hold that the power of haumain and manmat is destroyed by praising the name of God and by unselfish service to others. For example during the time I lived in the gurdwara complex in Bangkok, a man considered to be the epitome of virtue in the community was an extremely wealthy person who came to the temple each morning long before sunrise and washed on his hands and knees the numerous stairs leading up to the main sanctuary. There were many, many stairs. Members of the Bangkok congregation were often blood donors, provided disaster relief in and around the city to both Sikhs and non-Sikhs, and were in general good corporate citizens.

Some principal proscriptions for Khalsa Sikhs include that body hair must not be cut or shaven, neither tobacco nor intoxicants can be used, *halal* (ritually slaughtered meat) is forbidden, and adultery is prohibited.

The ultimate goal of a Sikh is *sahaj.*

sahaj—Salvation; union with God; the result of devotional worship. Many Sikhs believe that until sahaj occurs an individual will continue in samsara.

The *gurdwara* is central to the life of a Sikh community.

gurdwara—Sikh temple and meeting place. The gurdwara houses the main worship area and is the location of the Holy Granth. A gurdwara also contains the langar.

The Golden Temple at Amritsar

The Golden Temple (*Swarnamandir*) is also variously known among Sikhs as *Harimandir* (Temple of God) and *Darbar Sahib* (Court Divine). Its dramatic and often bloody history functions within the context of Sikhism to underscore for Sikhs the powerful sacramental and political symbolism of the place in Sikh worldview. For many Sikhs the Golden Temple represents an important locus of Sikh culture.

In early times the area of the Golden Temple was thickly forested. The present tank was a natural pool regarded as imbued with spiritual significance by indigenous peoples in the region. According to local lore, Sakyamuni Buddha visited the place that had been a destination for Buddhist pilgrims. Around 1532 C.E. Guru Nanak lived near the pool. In 1577 the area around the pool was acquired by Guru Ram Dass who ordered the dredging and expansion of the pool and named it Amritsar (Pool of Nectar/Immortality). The first temple to occupy the site was completed around 1604. During the lifetime of Guru Arjan the temple prospered and attracted numerous pilgrims. Under Guru Hargobind strict rules of behavior within the gurdwara precincts were laid down, and the following are examples of prohibited activity: gambling, tobacco use, defecating and/or urinating outside of prescribed areas, and inappropriate interaction with women. Hargobind and the Sikhs were driven from Amritsar by the Mughal army in 1628, and the temple was desecrated. The holy precincts were reclaimed under the leadership of the tenth Guru, but the temple was lost again to the Mughals in 1738 when the Commandant of Amritsar established within the sacred site a police station, civil court, and stables. According to Sikh tradition the most sacred areas of the temple were used as a dancing hall and venue for wild parties, rumored actions that culminated in an unsuccessful attack by the Sikhs and resulted in severe persecutions against them which reached their peak in the *ghallughara* (holocaust) of March 1746 when many Sikhs were beheaded, copies of the *Granth* destroyed, and the holy tank was filled with foul rubbish. Worse still was to come with the fourth Afgan invasion in 1757 when the troops of Ahmed Shah Abdali hacked their way to Delhi. Their bloody conquest was interrupted by a cholera outbreak forcing them to attempted to retreat homeward with their booty. The Sikhs ambushed a least one sizable treasure caravan, but the action caused Abddali to retaliate by blowing up the temple at Amritsar and defiling the tank with the ruins and the bloody entrails of slaughtered cows. Sikh reaction was swift, heroic, and severe, and, in a ferocious battle the Sikhs under the leadership of the battle's great martyr Baba Dip Singh, the invaders were expelled and the gurdwara was rebuilt only to survive until 1762 when once again Abdali invaded and butchered nearly 30,000 Sikhs in the *Vada Ghallughara* (Great Massacre). Yet again Abdali retreated in order to quell internal disturbances in Afganistan, and again the Sikhs rebuilt the temple. In 1764 the persistent Abdali invaded for the seventh time, easily retook the gurdwara, and once again blew it up and filled the tank with the intestines and blood of herds of cows. By 1765 the Shah withdrew with the fruits of conquest, and the Sikhs resolved yet again to rebuild their gurdwara. In 1799 Armritsar came under the control of the great Sikh leader Maharaja Ranjit Singh who undertook a major building program to improve Amritsar and the temple. The Sikhs remained in control of the Golden Temple until the British Raj assumed control in 1846 and oversaw the administration of the gurdwara until 1925 when it was turned over to a Sikh group. During the violent events surrounding the Partition (the political division of the Punjab following the British withdrawal resulting in the western portion of the region being given to Pakistan and the eastern region given to India) the Golden Temple was protected by Sikhs and spared from destruction. In recent Indian history the Harimandir was assaulted by troops under orders of the Prime Minister Indira Ghandi in 1984, an action that resulted in her assassination at the hands of a Sikh bodyguard.

The Harimandir is a significant and arresting aesthetic achievement. It rests on a platform rising from a tank (pool). A promenade called the *Parikarma* encircles the tank and serves to facilitate and mark the path for ritual circumambulation. Devotees reach the temple via a marble causeway passing an arch called *Darshani Darwaza* (Gate of Prayer). The temple itself is a square marble structure consisting of two stories. Its exterior walls are covered with gold-plated copper sheets and cover too the central low fluted dome as well as the four kiosks fitted with cupolas seated upon each of the corners of the roof. The lower walls extending six feet from the base are decorated with white marble and inlaid with precious and semiprecious stones. There are four carved ivory doors corresponding with the cardinal points of the compass.

The interior ground floor consists of a single hall and galleries whose walls are faced with decorated marble slabs inlaid with metal, precious stones, and *mohra qashi* (fresco painting). It is at the center of the hall under a jeweled canopy that the *Granth* is installed for veneration from early in the morning until late at night.

The principal feature of the upper story is the *Parkash Asthan* (Place of Light) where the holy *Granth* is kept surrounded by the *Shish Mahal* (Hall of Mirrors). According to Sikh tradition the Hall was originally a pavillion used by the Gurus as a meditation place. Today the highly decorated space is used for *Akand Path* (Perpetual Recitation of the *Adi Granth Sahib*).

It is useful to note that the Golden Temple is the axis of a constellation of structures that function in various ways to serve the sacred and mundane missions of the Sikhs and is a model for many gurdwaras around the world in the Sikh diaspora.

10

The Jains

I n this brief chapter we shall address some of the principal characteristics of Jainism, a religious tradition that is relatively unknown and
generally not well understood in the West. Perhaps one reason for their
"obscurity" is their small numbers. Scholars suggest that there are but a
very few million Jains, less than one percent of the total population of
India where most of them reside. On the other hand, the Jains tend to
attract the attention of students of Indian culture due to what many
Westerners perceive as "exotic" beliefs and practices.

Jain Cosmology and Worldview

Jains perceive the cosmos as being like a gigantic human figure.
Humans and other earth bound creatures are at the waist. Below the
waist are several levels of "purgatories." Above the waist are "heavenly"
places inhabited by gods. (Note that Jains both normatively and operatively believe in the existence and powers of Hindu gods; however, the
deities are held to be of less importance in terms of salvation. The roles
of the gods in Jainism are to provide assistance in more mundane
affairs. Jainism is essentially a nontheistic religion wherein the forces of
karma and samsara are operative and determinative.) Above the vast
cosmic figure's head is the sublime and exalted locus of the perfected
souls, and it is to enter this state of perfection, where samsara and suffering ends, that Jains aspire.

Jains claim that their religion is the world's oldest religion and that
it predates Hinduism and Buddhism; however, many scholars offer

arguments to the contrary, and it is beyond the scope of this book to consider these arguments here. Instead we shall endeavor to appreciate this religious tradition from a more emic perspective and focus on what Jains appear to believe and do.

As we have already noted, Jainism is normatively atheistic. Operatively Jain temples contain images of Hindu deities whom many Jains venerate and petition for boons and interventions. Jains look to Brahmin (Hindu) priests to consecrate major events in the life cycle, e.g. weddings.

The law of karma looms large in the belief system, and the Jain emphasis on aestheticism can be more immediately appreciated in terms of karma and its nature. Hindus and Buddhists view karma as a law or "force" that operates according to a kind of cause and effect principle, but Jains believe it is an actual particular substance consisting of matter which sticks to the soul and that moksha can be reached if a man (women cannot reach moksha in their present incarnations as females) is able to through spiritual means to liberate his own soul *(jiva).*

Jiva—"Soul."

The soul's natural state includes of a kind of awareness/ "knowing" or transcendent omniscience. In its worldly state the soul's natural knowledge is encumbered and therefore imperfect. Jains believe in several levels through which the soul might transmigrate in accordance with the forces of good or bad karma. Thus the soul may exist in a hierarchical continuum from vegetable, insect, animal, human being in "hell" or else in heaven, etc.

Jains believe that harmful karma "weighs" down the soul thereby preventing it from ascending into liberated bliss and perfect knowledge. Heavy or negative karma is caused by selfish or cruel actions, but it can also be created through carelessness (for this reason Jain aesthetics filter their drinking water in order not to accidently ingest an insect). Jain karmic doctrine holds that heavy karma is neutralized or dissipated by good deeds that produce good karma. Further, spiritual progress is enhanced by aesthetic suffering which is also held to be efficacious in dispelling heavy karma

Jains. Jinas, and Tirthamkaras

What is a Jain? A Jain is literally a person who follows the *Jina:*

Jain—Follower of the Victor or "Jina" (Conqueror). The title "Jina" also refers specifically to Vardhamana, the last of the great Jain teachers who is more widely known as Mahavira.

Who, then, is the Victor/Conqueror? The Victor(s)/Conqueror(s) are the *tirthamkaras*.

Tirthamkara(s)—"Ford Finders;" those who orginally crossed over/transcended the river of life and found release/moksha from samsara and karmic matter.

Jains believe that there were 24 tirthamkaras beginning with Risabha who lived 8.4 million years; however, we will limit our discussion here to the person who Jains believe was the most recent and final tirthamkara, i.e., Vardhamana aka **Mahavira** who holds a highly significant place in the Jain tradition.

Mahavira (599 B.C.E.–527 B.C.E.) was probably a historical person who according to both Jain and Buddhist tradition reportedly engaged in disputes with the Buddha Sakyamuni. Indeed, he is often referred to in Buddhist scriptures where he is described as an opponent of the Buddha. Mahavira's biography is somewhat similar to that of Sakyamuni Buddha. He was a ksyatria "prince," raised and educated as a son of wealth and privilege, who renounced family life at age of 28 in order to become a wandering ascetic in pursuit of moksha via the practice of severe asceticism. The "way" he chose led him to renounce clothing (he went about naked until his death). He followed the spiritual path of the previous Jina and embarked upon a lengthy fast and at the age of 40 he achieved moksha thereby becoming a jina (conqueror) and perfected soul liberated forever from the effects of karma. He spent the remaining 30 years of his life promoting his beliefs and teaching his followers. It is significant to note here that Jains believe that jina are able to achieve moksha in this life as did Mahavira. Jain doctrine holds that a kind of "residual" karma holds them in the earthly sphere but that this residual karma can be sloughed off by fasting and penance. Once the remaining karma is gone the soul is free to rise above the highest heavens into the eternal bliss that is nirvana. In Mahavira's case the karmic residue was shed as a result of his voluntary starvation in village near Patna, the town of his birth.

Scriptures and basic tenets

The Jain scriptures are based on an oral tradition of teachings believed to have originated with Mahavira. In the 13th century these teachings were codified into twelve sections. Jain scripture is called **Agams**. The various Jain sects accept or reject to varying degrees the Agams. Among the sects are the;

> *Digambaras* (sky clad)—who reject clothing.
>
> *Svetambaras* (white clad)—who do not reject clothing.

There are of course numerous important distinctions between the sects, but these considerations are beyond the scope of this book.

Earlier we discussed something of the nature of Jain karmic doctrine and will continue now to discuss it further. Please recall that "heavy" karma can be dissipated quickly by good karma resulting from good deeds, fasting, and penance or other voluntary suffering perceived as "good" according to Jain beliefs. But what more specifically is the source of heavy karma? Jains hold that harmful karma results from among other things worldly attachments to things, "false" beliefs (such as the tenets of Buddhism), greed, anger, and the like.

Jains believe that humans must urgently and rigorously make every effort to attain salvation. For the Jains this means acquiring the Three Jewels which consist of (1) Right Knowledge (ie. Jainism); (2) Right Faith (believing in the Way of the Jains); and (3) Right Conduct (practicing Jainism). Central to the tenets of Right Conduct is the practice of *ahimsa*, an ethical principle which we have considered in our discussion of Buddhism. For Jains, ahimsa is as in Buddhism "nonviolence" and entails the avoidance of any possible injury to living entities of every sort. Because ahimsa is essential if one is to avoid negative karma and/or obtain the spiritual benefits of good karma, Jains take and implement vows committing them to Right Conduct including ahimsa. It is in the interest of practicing ahimsa that Jains practice strict vegatarianism, do not engage in occupations that cause harm to entities including nonorganic ones like earth, wood, metals, etc, and may wear gauze masks so as not to accidentally ingest an insect or injure the air through the very act of breathing, gasping, or gulping.

In that Jainism is largely monastic in orientation, the sangha of monks and nuns is a significant institution. Leadership roles within the sangha are filled by **acaryas** (spiritual teachers/supervisors who oversee meditation and discipline) and teachers who are in charge of educating members and laity in scripture and mundane subjects.

Central to the Way of the Jains are vows taken by both members of the sangha and the laity. The vows for laity may be permanent or temporary and are less restrictive than those taken by members of the sangha Vows taken by the Jain ascetic (sadhu) are the most severe and restrictive. The purpose of the vows from the normative perspective of Jains are to promote health, avoid to the degree practicable karma, and to aid in the expiation of heavy karma.

Devout Jain lay persons and those within the sangha begin their day with personal devotions. Jain homes have domestic shrines, and devotions and venerations are also offered in temples housing images of the tirthankaras and Hindu deities.

APPENDIX

Sacrifice and Service: An Observation on the Religion of Nanak and the Hindu Tradition

By
Jack Sikora

While it is generally accepted that Sikhism is a distinct religion there remains a shadow upon its origins, i.e. the notion that it was, and therefore continues to be, a syncretism, the product of an amalgamation of Hinduism and Islam. In this essay I hold that the founder of the Sikh religion, Guru Nanak, a pious Hindu deeply effected by the spiritual currents of Islam that surrounded him and were an inherent part of his worldview, employed essential idioms from both the Hindu Way and Islam in order to both perceive and communicate the nature of the spiritual call to which he was compelled to surrender. On the other hand what we have of Nanak's actual words comes to us through scripture, to a lesser extent, and later exegesis to a greater extent. In the case of the latter what we may have before us is less the language of the founding Guru and more the message of the tradition itself including that of its apologists and political "spin doctors." In either case what we have is the voice of the tradition, a voice that speaks in the idiom of the Hindus and Muslims; therefore, at least a cursory analysis of the nature of the idioms is potentially useful in developing a sense of one way in which we might appreciate Sikhism as a unique religion. Specifically, I believe that Nanak used the metaphors, symbols, and scriptures of the Hindus and Muslims as idioms to communicate the Sikh Way and that the idiom is just that, an idiom and not a doctrine. Sikhism's right to its claim that it is distinct is a legitimate one.

The sacred scriptures of the Hindus document both the evolutionary and sometimes revolutionary changes in principal modes of worship as the tradition transitioned from Arya religion, to the Brahmanical tradition, to Hinduism in all of its myriad guises. Beginning with the *yajna* fire sacrifice and tracing the principal popular mode of worship through yoga, *karmamarga*, and *bahakti* the essence of sacrificial energy (fire, heat, sound vibrations, offering—including that of the individual himself as demanded by *dharma*, etc) remains thematic. The sacrifice is a principle idiom.

The phenomenon of the sacrifice as a mode of worship emerged as a principal mode of worship in the Vedic Age (1500–1000 B.C.E.) where it was, among other aspects of Arya religion, central to the rites performed in the *yajna* cult. The rites were focused around a fire and were offered in honor of one or more deities. As the fire burned, Vedic hymns and/or other mantras were uttered by a priest assisted by other priests who played various specialized roles to ensure the efficacy of the rites. The fire sacrifice and its allied rituals provided a locus of hospitality for the gods luring them within human reach. In addition to the sacred utterances and their resulting sacred sounds was the sacrificial offering of *ghee, soma,* grain and the like. The oblations were carried to the gods by Agni, god of fire and messenger to the gods. Thus the *yajna* sacrifice provided a means of spiritual correspondence between human and gods. Its profane objectives were to obtain boons by lavishing the *deva* with praise, offerings, and the holiest of sounds. Patrons of the sacrifice sought to ensure the provision of sons, cows, long life, etc. On the level of the sacred the sacrifice was ultimately understood by pundits and priests as a kind of ultimate reality, the metaphysical axis of creation.

The Upanishadic Age (500 B.C.E.–200 C.E.) gave rise to additional perceptions of the sacrificial ideal while leaving its essential meaning intact. The sacrifice was no longer exclusively a ritual performed around three fires by priests. It could be understood as personal attitude and action or knowledge as described, for example, in the *Chandogya Upanishad*, VIII, v.1: "*What is commonly called sacrifice is really the chaste life of* [the] *student of sacred knowledge... What is commonly called sacrificial offering is really the chaste life of a student of sacred knowledge... 1* The Upanishadic concept of sacrifice included perceiving and practicing it under the guise of yoga as described in the *Svetasvatara Upanishad*, I, v.14: "*Make thy body the lower fire-stick... Om the upper: Make use of meditation like the friction... Then whilt thou see God, like hidden... fire... 2*

With the emergence of the *Bhagavad-Gita* as an increasingly popular devotional guide, the internalized and personal yogic sacrifice is presented as *karmayoga*. In Chapter II, v. 50, Krishna instructs Arjana that "*Whoso is integrated... Discards both good and evil works... Brace yourself... for this Yoga! Yoga is skill in performing works. 3* In 18, v. 46, Krishna instructs that "*By dedicating the work that is proper... To Him who is the source of all beings' activity... By whom this whole universe was spun... A man attains perfection and success.4* Thus the sacrifice as duty facilitates the correspondence of man and the Divine. It is significant to appreciate that the sacrificial act here is not a simple surrender of ego. Instead the devotee transforms his adherence to his *dharma* into the metaphorical execution of the sacrificial rite.

In both yoga and karmayoga the mode of worship is governed by the belief in the efficacy of the essence of the sacrifice. Specifically, the concept of sacrifice is the paradigm that in each case establishes the framework for and fixes the parameters in the mode of worship. Whether actual or metaphorical the function of the sacrifice is to facilitate and ultimately actualize a correspondence between man and the

Divine. This correspondence is not a simple surrender of ego, i.e. the actor-petitioner-seeker-devotee becomes himself the metaphorical sacrificial victim. The idiom, laden with traditional symbols and grounded in language, is the sacrifice, and the sacrifice is the essence of Hinduism. In the Hindu tradition the student may be called to transform his chaste life; the yogi is instructed to make his very body the fire stick; those bound by the proscriptions and prescriptions of dharma offer their ascribed station, the social "self;" in puja the devotee summoned to worship his chosen God divides and shares himself in bhakti. In each case the sacrifice is consummated, and it is its idiom that calls and conditions the follower's response.

In the teachings of Nanak as we have them in scripture and exegesis what might appear to be the sacrificial idiom is present, i.e. the actor is called to action and transformation from the familiar to the sacred. For example, when the future Guru's father suggested that he become a farmer, Nanak "replied:" *Make thy body the field, good works the seed, irrigate with God's name:/Make they heart the cultivator; God will germinate in they heart, and thou shalt thus obtain the dignity of nirvan.* 5 When his father suggested that the boy should become a shop keeper, Nanak retorted: *Make the knowledge that life is frail they shop, the true Name they stock-in-trade;/Make meditation and contemplation they piles of vessels; put true Name into them.* 6 Early in his public ministry Nanak was brought before the Governor's Qazi to explain his teaching that "There is no Hindu and no Muslim." He sought to convey his message to Muslims in these words: *Make kindness thy mosque, sincerity thy prayer carpet, What is just and lawful thy Quran./ Modesty thy circumcision, civility thy fasting, so shalt thou be a Musalman;/Make right conduct thy kaaba, truth thy spiritual guide, good works thy creed and thy prayer,/ The will of God thy rosary...7* In each of these instances, while the idiom is Hindu, it does not imply sacrifice. Nanak's call to transformation does not constitute an offering but a new understanding. Nanak's Way does not require that the hearer become a victim but a believer and a doer of the Word. In this way the religion of the Sikhs departs significantly from Hinduism.

End Notes

R.C. Zaehner., ed. *Hindu Scripture.* (New York: Dutton, 1968), p.125.
Ibid. p.205
Ibid. p.259
Ibid. p.322
Macauliffe, Max Arthur. *The Sikh Religion* Vol. 1. (Delhi: S. Chand and Company, 1963), p.21.
Ibid. p.23
Ibid. p.38

References

Hopkins, Thomas J. *The Hindu Religious Tradition.* Encino and Belmont: CA: Dickenson Publishing Company, 1971.

Macauliffe, Max Arthur. *The Sikh Religion* Vol. 1. New Delhi: S. Chand and Company, 1963.

McLeod, Hew. *Sikhism.* New York: Penguin Putnam, 1997.

Singh, Kushwant. *The Sikhs Today: Their Religion, History, Culture, Customs and Way of Life.* Bombay: Orient Longmans, 1959.

Trumpp, Ernest., trans. *The Adi Granth.* New Delhi: Munshiram Mandhardal, 1970.

Zaehner, R.C., ed. *Hindu Scriptures.* New York: Dutton, 1968.

Bibliography

Akira, Hirakawa. *A History of Indian Buddhism From Sakyamuni to Early Mahayana.* Honolulu: University of Hawaii Press, 1990.

Atkins, A. G. *The Ramayana of Tulsidas.* 2 vols. Calcutta: Birila Academy of Art and Culture, 1966.

Banerjee, S. C. *Dharma Sutras: A Study in Their Origins and Development.* Calcutta: Punthi Pustak, 1962.

Barua, Benimadhab. *The History of Pre-Buddhist Philosophy.* Delhi: Motilal Banarsidass, 1970.

Basham, A. L. *The Wonder That Was India.* New York: Grove Press, 1954.

Beaver, R. Pierce, et al, eds. *Eerdman's Handbook to the World's Religions.* Grand Rapids, Michigan: William B. Eerdmans Publishing Company, 1982.

Bechert, Heinz and Richard Gombrich. *The World of Buddhism.* New York: Facts on File, 1984.

Berger, Peter L. *The Sacred Canopy: Elements of a Sociological Theory of Religion.* Garden City: NY: Doubleday, 1967.

Bercholz, Samuel and Sherab Chodzin Kohn, eds. *An Introduction to the Buddha and His Teachings.* New York: Barnes and Noble, 1997.

Beyer, S. *The Buddhist Experience: Sources and Interpretations.* Encino and Belmont, CA: Dickenson, 1974.

Bharati, Agehananda. *The Tantric Tradition.* Garden City, NY: Doubleday Anchor, 1970.

_____, ed. *The Realm of the Extrahuman: Agents and Audiences.* The
Hague: Mouton. 1976.

Bhatt, G. H., ed. *The Valmiki Ramayana.* Baroda: Oriental Institute,
1960.

Blair, Chauncey. *Heat in the Rig Veda and Atharva Veda.* New Haven:
American Oriental Society, 1961.

Bowen, John R. *Religions in Practice: An Approach to the Anthropology of
Religion.* 2nd ed. Boston: Allyn and Bacon.

Brereton, Bonnie Pacala. *The Phra Malai Legend in Thai Buddhist Literature.* Tempe: Arizona State university Press, 1994.

Burke, Kenneth. *Language as Symbolic Action.* Berkeley: University of
California Press, 1966.

Chartier, Roger. *Cultural History: Between Practices and Representa-
tions.* Oxford: Polity Press, 1988.

Chaudhury, Uma. *The Social Dimensions of Early Buddhism.* Delhi:
Oxford University Press, 1987.

Chakravati, Uma. The Social Dimensions of Early Buddhism, Oxford:
Oxford University Press, 1987.

Coedes, Ggeorge. *The Indianized States of Southeast Asia.* Honolulu:
University of Hawaii Press, 1968.

Conze, Edward. *Buddhist Thought in India.* London: Allen and
Unwin, 1962.

_____. *Buddhism: Its Essence and Development*. New York. Harper Torchbooks, 1959.

Dayal, Har. *The Bodhisattva Doctrine in Buddhist Sanskrit Literature*. Delhi: Motilal Banarsidass, 1970.

De Bary, William T., ed. *The Buddhist Tradition In India, China, and Japan*. New York: Modern Library, 1969.

Dharma, Krishna. *Ramayana: India's Immortal Tale of Adventure, Love, and Wisdom*. Badger, CA: Torchlight Publishing Company, 2000.

During, S. ed. *The Cultural Studies Reader*. London: Routledge, 1993.

Durkheim, Emile. *The Elementary Forms of the Religious Life*. trans. J.W. Swain. New York: Free Press, (1912) 1968.

Dutt, Romesh C. *The Ramayana and The Mahabharata*. New York: Dutton Everyman's Library, 1969.

Dutt, Sukumar. *Buddhist Monks and Monastries of India: Their History and Their Contribution to Indian Culture*. London: Allen and Unwin, 1962.

Edgerton, Franklin, trans. *The Bagavad Gita*. Cambridge, MA: Harvard University Press, 1985.

Embree, Ainslee T. *The Hindu Tradition*. New York: Random House, 1972.

_____, ed. *The Encyclopedia of Religion* (16 vols.). New York: Macmillan, 1987.

Fenton, John, et al. *Religions of Asia*. New York: St. Martin's Press, 1993.

Geertz, Clifford. "Ethos, Worldview, and the Analysis of Sacred Symbols." In *The Interpretation of of Cultures*. New York: Basic Books, 1973.

Gokhale, Balkrishna Govind. *Buddhism and Asoka*. Baroda: Padmaja Publications, 1948.

Griffith, Ralph T. H., *The Ramayana of Valmiki*, 3rd ed. Varanas: The Chowkhamba Sanskrit Series Office, 1963.

Hall, Edward T., *The Silent Language*. New York: Doubleday, 1959.

Hargrove, Barbara. *The Sociology of Religion: Classical and Contemporary Approaches*, 2nd ed. Arlington Heights, IL: Harlan Davidson, 1989.

Harris, Marvin. *The Rise of Anthropological Theory: A History of Theories of Culture*. New York: Thomas Y. Crowell Company, 1968.

Hastings, James. *Encyclopedia of Religion and Ethics*. 13 vols. New York: Charles Scribner's Sons, 1908–1927.

Herman, A. L. *A Brief Introduction to Hinduism: Religion, Philosophy, and Ways of Liberation*. Boulder, CO: Westview Press, 1991.

Hill, William Douglas P. *The Holy Lake of the Acts of Rama*. London: Oxford university Press, 1952.

Hopkins, Thomas J. *The Hindu Religious Tradition*. Encino, CA: Dickinson Publishing Company, 1971.

Ishi, Yoneo. *Sangha, State, and Society: Thai Buddhism in History*. Honolulu: University of Hawaii Press, 1988.

Jaini, Padmanabh S. *The Jaina Path of Purification*. Berkeley: University of California Press, 1979.

Kabilsingh, Chatsumarn. *Thai Women In Buddhism*. Berkeley, CA: Parallax Press, 1991.

Kalra, Balwant Singh. *Brief History of Sikh Gurdwaras in Thailand*. Bangkok: Siri Guru Singh Sabha.

Keith, Arthur Berridale. *The Religion and Philosophy of the Vedas and Upanishads*. Harvard Oriental Series, nos. 31–32. Cambridge: Harvard University Press, 1925.

Keyes, Charles F. *The Golden Peninsula: Culture and Adaptation in Mainland Southeast Asia*. New York: Macmillan, 1977.

Khan, Benjamin. *The Concept of Dharma In Valmiki Ramayana*. Delhi: Munshi Ram Manohar Lal, 1965.

Klima, Alan. *The Funeral Casino: Meditation, Massacre, and Exchange With the Dead in Thailand*. Princeton: Princeton University Press, 2002.

Kosambi, D. D. *The Culture and Civilization of Ancient India in Historical Outline*. London: Vikas Publications, 1965.

Kurtz, Lester. *Gods in the Global Village: The World's Religions in Sociological Perspective*. Thousand

Oaks, CA: Pine Forge, 1995.

Laidlaw, James. *Riches and Renunciation: Religion, Economy, and Society Among the Jains*. New York: Oxford University Press, 1995.

Lemert, Charles. *Social Theory: The Multicultural and Classic Readings*, 2nd ed. Boulder, CO: Westview Press, 1999.

Lessa, William A. and Evon Z. Vogt, eds. *Reader in Comparative Religion: An Anthropological Approach*, 4th ed. New York: Harper and Row, 1979.

Lingat, Robert. *The Classical Law of India.* Berkeley: University of California Press, 1973.

Macauliffe, Max A. *The Sikh Religion: Its Gurus, Sacred Writings and Authors* (6 vols.). Oxford: Clarendon Press, 1909.

MacDonell, A. A. *The Vedic Mythology.* Varanasi: Indological Book House, 1963.

Macfie, J. M. *The Ramayana of Valmiki: A Summary.* Madras, The Christian Literature Society for India, 1923.

McLeod, Hew. *Sikhism.* New York: Penguin Books, 1997.

Metcalf, Thomas R. ed. *Modern India: An Interpretive Anthology.* London: The Macmillan Company, 1971.

Nelson, Walter Henry. *Buddha: His Life and Teaching.* New York: Jeremy P. Tarcher/Putnam, 1996.

Oldenberg, H. *The Buddha: His Life, His Order, His Doctrine.* Varanasi: Indological Book House, 1971.

Powell, Barbara. *Windows Into the Infinite: A Guide to the Hindu Scriptures.* Fremont, CA: Jain Publishing Company, 1996.

Prebish, Charles. *Buddhist Monastic Discipline: The Sanskrit Pratimoksksa Sutras of the Mahasanghikas an Mulasarvastivadins.* University Park, PA: Pennsylvania State University Press, 1975.

Rahula, Walpola. *What The Buddha Taught.* New York: Grove Press, 1959.

Reynolds, Frank E. *The Buddhist Monkhood in Nineteenth Century Thailand.* Ann Arbor: University of Michigan, 1973.

Renou, Louis. *Religions of Ancient India.* London: Athlone Press, 1953.

Roberts, Keith. *Religion in Sociological Perspective.* Chicago: Dorsey Press, 1984.

Robinson, Richard H. and Willard Johnson. *The Buddhist Religion,* 3rd ed. Belmont, CA: Wadsworth, 1982.

Sidhu, G.S. *Introduction to Sikhism.* Gravesend, United Kingdom: The Sikh Missionary Society U.K., 1973.

Singh, Kushwant. *A History of the Sikhs* (2 vols.). Princeton, NJ: Princeton University Press, 1963, 1966.

Singh, Patwant. *The Golden Temple.* New Delhi: Time Books International, 1988.

Singh, S. Gurubakhash, trans. *Sri Japji of Sri Guru Nanank Devji.* Bombay: The Veekay Weekly.

Singh, Vir Bhai Sahib. *Sri Kirtan Sohila Sahib.* Amritsar: M/s. Singh Brothers

Smart, Ninian. *Religions of Asia.* Englewood Cliffs, NJ: 1993.

Smith, H. Daniel and Jack Sikora. *A Dharma Reader* (unpublished manuscript). 1974.

Smith, H. Daniel. *Selections from Vedic Hymns.* Berkeley, CA: McCutchan Publishing Corporation, 1968.

Smith, Huston. *The World's Religions: Our Great Wisdom Traditions.* San Francisco: Harper Collins, 1991.

Snelling, John. *The Buddhist Handbook: The Complete Guide to Buddhist Schools, Teaching, Practice, and History.* Rochester, VT: Inner Traditions, 1991.

Snodgrass, Adrian. *The Symbolism of the Stupa*. Ithaca, NY: Cornell University Southeast Asian Studies Program, 1985.

Spiro, Melford E. *Buddhism and Society: A Geat Tradition and Its Burmese Vicissitudes,* 2nd ed. Berkeley: University of California Press, 1982.

Strong, John. *The Legend of King Asoka: A Study and Translation of the Asokavadana*. Princeton, NJ: Princeton University Press, 1983.

Swearer, Donald K. *The Buddhist World of Southeast Asia*. Albany: State University of New York Press, 1995.

Tambiah, S.J. *The Buddhist Saints of the Forest and the Cult of Amulets: A Study in Charisma, Hagiography, Sectarianism, and Millenial Buddhism*. Cambridge: Cambridge University Press, 1984.

_____. *Buddhism and the Spirit Cults of Northeast Thailand*. Cambridge: Cambridge University Press, 1970.

Trumpp, Ernest. *The Adi Granth*. New Delhi: Munshirman Mandharal, 1970.

Tyler, Stephen A. *India: An Anthropological Introduction*. Prospect Heights, IL: Waveland Press, 1973.

Upsak, C. S., *Dictionary of Early Buddhist Monastic Terms*. Varanasi: Bharati Prakashan, 1975.

Weber, Max. *The Protestant Ethic and the Spirit of Capitalism*. New York: Scribner's, 1958.

Welbon, Guy. *Buddhist Nirvana and Its Western Interpreters*. Chicago: University of Chicago Press, 1968.

Wijayaratna, Mohan. *Buddhist Monastic Life*. Cambidge: Cambridge University, 1990.

Williams, Paul. *Mahayana Buddhism: The Doctrinal Foundations.* London and New York: Routledge, 1989.

Zaehner, Richard C. *Hinduism.* New York: Oxford University Press, 1962.

Zaehner, Richard C. (ed.). *Hindu Scriptures.* New York: Dutton, 1968.

Zimmer, Heinrich. *Myths and Symbols in Indian Art and Civilization.* New York: Harper, 1946.

About the Author

Jack Sikora is Senior Adjunct Lecturer in Social Sciences at Western Connecticut State University (WCSU) and a visiting faculty member in the Graduate Liberal Studies Program at Wesleyan University. His academic specialties include Anthropology, Sociology, and Asian Religions. In addition to core courses at WCSU he teaches "Intercultural Communication;" "Religions in India;" and "Buddhism." He has taught in Saudi Arabia and Thailand.

0-595-24712-1